PLEASANTON
CALIFORNIA
❖ A Brief History ❖

KEN MACLENNAN *for*
Pleasanton's Museum on Main

Published by The History Press
Charleston, SC 29403
www.historypress.net

Copyright © 2014 by Museum on Main
All rights reserved

Cover images: Alameda County Fairgrounds courtesy of Mike Sedlak, Digital Sight; Pleasanton town band courtesy of Museum on Main.

First published 2014

Manufactured in the United States

ISBN 978.1.62619.353.6

Library of Congress CIP data applied for.

Notice: The information in this book is true and complete to the best of our knowledge. It is offered without guarantee on the part of the author or The History Press. The author and The History Press disclaim all liability in connection with the use of this book.

All rights reserved. No part of this book may be reproduced or transmitted in any form whatsoever without prior written permission from the publisher except in the case of brief quotations embodied in critical articles and reviews.

CONTENTS

Acknowledgements	5
Introduction	7
PART I: BEFORE PLEASANTON	
The Earliest Residents, circa 5000 BCE–1769 CE	9
The Mission Era, 1769–1834	15
Ranchos and Ranchers, 1834–1862	21
PART II: PLEASANTON SMALL	
A New Community: Unincorporated Pleasanton, 1862–1894	37
Progressive Pleasanton: The Booster Years, 1894–1920	70
Prohibition, Depression and War: Pleasanton, 1920–1945	94
PART III: PLEASANTON GROWING	
So This Is Growth, 1945–1970	119
Crisis and Renewal, 1970–1990	136
Into the Twenty-first Century	148
Notes	153
Bibliography	165
Index	171
About the Author	175

ACKNOWLEDGEMENTS

Even a brief history such as this one cannot be written without incurring numerous debts of gratitude. It is unlikely that the following list covers them all; the author's apologies go to those who have been inadvertently omitted.

My first group of debts is to those researchers and historians of the Valley whose earlier spadework has made my own writing so much easier: Beverly Ales, Terry Berry, Barbara Bunshah, Robert Delgado, Douglas Greenberg, Herbert Hagemann Jr., Phil Henry, Anne Homan, David Kiehn, Ted Klenk, Bob and Pat Lane, Randall Milliken, Janet Newton, Gene Pons, Mary Jo Wainwright and the membership of the Livermore-Amador Genealogical Society.

The second group of debts is to the peers and colleagues who provided active support and assistance to this project. These begin with my fellow staff members: Executive Director Jim DeMersman, Director of Education Jen Amiel and Administrative Assistant Bonnie Fitzpatrick. They continue with Steve Minnear, whose advice and friendly interest were nearly as useful as his own work on the history of the Valley's military installations. Andy Galvan and Beverly Ortiz provided bibliographical advice on Ohlone history. Diane Curry at the Hayward Area Historical Society provided a key piece of fact checking. And extra credit goes to those members of the Museum on Main's redoubtable corps of volunteers who allowed me to subvert their time to this book's ends: Judy Rathbone Burt, Fiona Catalano, Jonathan Hamilton and James Wei, as well as board members Charles Huff, Sandra Jellison, Lynn Skarratt and Sandi Thorne.

A third group of debts is owed to the people who build and maintain the digital resources that allowed me to expand the reach of my research so broadly in so short a time. In particular, credit goes to University of California–Riverside's California Digital Newspaper Collection, a freely available trove of California journalism that provided valuable coverage of the late nineteenth- and early twentieth-century Valley.

The hunt for cover images took us far and wide, and I would like to thank Michelle Crose, Pamela Ott and Sean Welch of the City of Pleasanton, as well as Sue Post at the Pleasanton Downtown Association, for their aid in the search. I would also like to thank both the city and PDA for their longtime support of the Museum on Main.

Another debt I owe to The History Press, for giving us the opportunity to produce this book in the first place, and yet another to the museum's board of directors, which gave its blessing to the project when we pitched it.

The final group of debts is to the friends and family who patiently allowed me to become a near-complete hermit while I buried myself in this project. Foremost among these is my wife, Allison Angell, who provided emotional support, nudged me when I got lazy, took on much of my share of the housework and provided extensive constructive criticism of my drafts. To her, the love of my life, I dedicate this work.

INTRODUCTION

Today, Pleasanton is the "City of Planned Progress," home to more than seventy thousand people, best known in the Bay Area for corporate headquarters and tech industries, expensive houses, high-quality schools and the Alameda County Fairgrounds. A century and a half ago, however, it was little more than an idea—a real estate project in a Bay Area backwater, conceived to profit from the railroad's advance through the Amador-Livermore Valley. Whatever hopes its founders may have had, they could not possibly have expected the growth and prosperity that their town would eventually attain.

The Amador-Livermore Valley has been called "corridor country" because of its position as a relatively convenient route through California's Coastal Range between the San Francisco Bay Area and the great Central Valley. The pathways it provided between the Central Valley to the east, the Santa Clara Valley to the south and the bay shore region to the west made it a logical place for a leg of the transcontinental railroad. Access to the Bay Area, in particular, has been critical to the history of the Valley and to the success of the city of Pleasanton—all the more since railways have ceded pride of place to freeways and agriculture to information.

Similarly, water and waterways have played crucial roles in the history of both the city and the valley in which it lies. From the now-drained great tule marsh that provided Ohlone tribes in the western Valley with game and building material to the arroyos that drew water from the Coastal Range west across the Valley and then south into Alameda

Introduction

Creek to quench the thirst of Oakland and San Francisco, as well as the aqueducts, canals and pipelines that today maintain the Valley's place in California's complex and delicate water economy, the importance of water has never fallen far below the surface of events.

This work is intended to be a brief survey of Pleasanton's history rather than a definitive work; there remains plenty of room for further research and publication on the subject. It is thus better considered *a* history of Pleasanton than *the* history of Pleasanton, and it is offered in part with the hope that it will provide solid footing on which future work can build.

PART I

BEFORE PLEASANTON

The Earliest Residents, circa 5000 BCE–1769 CE

The earliest dated traces of a human presence in the Amador-Livermore Valley are estimated to be more than seven thousand years old.[1] However, it is possible that the earliest Californians entered the Valley before 10,000 BCE during their rapid spread through the region. These people moved frequently and traveled light, leaving little behind in the way of material culture.[2] They are primarily noted for Clovis-style projectile points—flaked stone arrowheads and spearheads well suited for hunting larger game. Because of Clovis points, archaeologists long characterized these first Californians as nomads living primarily on big game. However, it is much more likely that hunting mammoth and bear was part of a diversified subsistence strategy, one that included small game such as rabbit and squirrel, as well as collecting edible seeds and plants that required relatively little processing.[3]

This first wave of humans in California has been named "proto-Hokan" by anthropologists, who connect them to those tribes (both historic and present-day) speaking languages in the Hokan family. According to this theory, the Hokan peoples were pushed out of central California toward its margins between about 2500 BCE and 500 CE, by groups speaking Penutian languages; these Penutian-speakers were the ancestors of the

Ohlone, Miwok and other native groups encountered by the Spanish when they first reached the Bay Area and the Central Valley.[4]

Also around 2000 BCE, the archaeological record shows a change in subsistence strategies, as acorns became a staple of native diets. Unprocessed acorns are virtually inedible by humans due to high concentrations of tannins. In order to make them suitable for eating, they had to be cracked open and the contents of the seed ground into meal, which would then be thoroughly soaked to leach out the tannins. The resulting meal was usually cooked with water to make a mush or baked into bread. Before about 2500 BCE, this process usually required more effort than it was worth, and people almost certainly ate acorns only in times of need. But climatic change and population pressure made more accessible foods relatively scarce, and acorns could be stored for extended periods, which made them attractive despite the labor-intensive preparation process.[5]

Embracing the acorn did not merely require native Californians to spend more time on food preparation; it spurred more drastic changes as well. It created a new division of labor along more gendered lines, as women took charge of acorn storage and processing, leaving hunting and fishing to men.[6] It sparked technological changes; as storage containers and cooking vessels became increasingly important, basketry techniques adapted to fill those needs. The greater volume of grinding and milling likewise raised the prominence of stone mortars and pestles.[7] The acorn also restricted movement because it was impractical to carry a whole season's worth of acorns around as the group followed its other food sources, and the community had to be close enough to its stores of acorns when the time to reclaim them arose.[8] In most areas, including the Tri-Valley, permanent residence was still not an option, and people adopted shorter cyclical patterns of migration to make sustainable use of local food resources. In addition, they learned to use controlled burning as a means of managing the landscape. The fires they set helped control underbrush and scrub plants, encouraged the growth of seed plants that people ate and increased the grazing area available to deer and other animals that they hunted.

Although they now spent most of their lives in smaller areas with a more limited range of resources, Californians living after this "acorn revolution" maintained trade with neighboring groups to ensure access to useful or desirable materials not found in their home territories. Examples found in the Amador-Livermore Valley include olivella shells from the bay shore and obsidian from the Napa Valley.[9]

By about the tenth century, patterns of life in the Bay Area had settled into an equilibrium that would remain roughly stable until the Spanish began to colonize the area in earnest after 1769.[10] The particulars were highly dependent on local geography; tribes in similar environments tended to share similar practices despite differences in language—differences that were themselves blurred by multilingualism—and the everyday lives of Ohlone tribes in the Amador-Livermore Valley had more in common with those of Miwok- or Yokuts-speaking neighbors to their north and east than with Ohlone-speaking tribes on the bay shore or the seacoast.[11]

The Ohlone of the Valley at the Time of First Contact

Archaeologist and ethnohistorian Randall Milliken has identified seven tribes living in and around the Amador-Livermore Valley around the turn of the nineteenth century, all of them speaking the Chochenyo dialect of the Ohlone language: Causen (west, in the northern Sunol Valley), Seunen (northwest, around Dublin), Souyen (north-central, around Tassajara Creek), Ssaoam (northeast, around Brushy Peak–Altamont Pass), Luecha (southeast, around Corral Hollow and Arroyo Mocho), Taunen (southwest, southern Sunol Valley) and Pelnen (west-central, around Pleasanton).[12] These tribes occupied the northeast march of the Ohlone-language area, with Bay Miwok speakers in the valleys to their north and Yokuts speakers beyond the Coast Range to the east.

The tribe was the basic unit of social and political organization. (California archaeologists have historically used the term "tribelet," but like Randall Milliken, whose lead I follow in this instance, I'm not certain the distinction is significant enough to warrant the use of the more specific term.)[13] Consisting of several intermarried families and numbering between two and four hundred people altogether, a tribe controlled an area averaging about eight to twelve miles in diameter, usually dividing its population among villages of about sixty to ninety inhabitants.[14] The tribe pooled its labor resources to house and feed itself, defended its territory against outside incursions, maintained a common system of rituals and shared a body of mythology and stories that gave metaphysical weight to the relationship between the tribe and the land it called home. These stories often shared key features across the region, but the details were always firmly tied to the landscape of the tribe's home territory.[15]

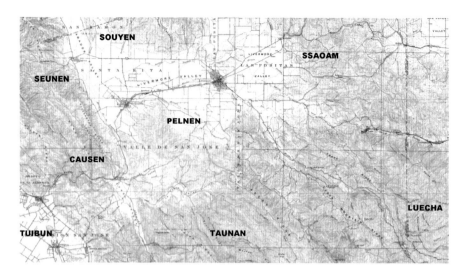

Tribal territories of the Amador-Livermore Valley at the time of Spanish contact, superimposed over the 1906 USGS maps of the Pleasanton and Tesla Quadrants. *After Milliken, A Time of Little Choice (1995).*

    Leadership of the tribe rested in a hereditary male chief, whose primary responsibilities apparently involved mediating disputes within the community, representing the tribe in interactions with guests and coordinating major activities such as warfare, religious ceremony and resource management.[16] The inner workings of tribal politics are not entirely clear, for European observers did not take sufficient interest in recording them at the time of contact and missionization eventually altered them beyond recognition. There is some evidence that tribal elders played an important role in advising chiefs, as well as passing traditions on to the next generation; these elders would have included men and women who specialized in the community's ritual lore: the dances, stories and other ceremonies that interpreted and managed the community's relationship with the powers of the universe. Beyond that, however, there is little that can be said for certain about the authority held by chiefs and elders or about the part that gender played in the distribution of authority and influence.

    Within their villages, the Ohlones generally lived in nuclear family units. Most marriages were monogamous, although some chiefs or other elite men may have had more than one wife thanks to the practice of diplomatic intertribal marriage.[17] Families lived in houses made from bundles of tule reed; these were easy to build and, when the time came to move on, even easier to tear down. The *temescal*, or sweat lodge, was an important feature of each village, serving key social and ritual purposes. Except in cold weather or for ritual purposes, men went more or less nude (or covered themselves in mud for a little extra insulation); women wore skirts or aprons of reed fibers.[18] When the temperature dropped, both genders wore capes or cloaks of rabbit skin or feathers.[19]

Gathering and processing plant foods was women's work, as was basketry and the care of young children. In addition to acorns, tribes in the Valley collected a variety of berries (blackberry, elderberry, gooseberry, madrone, strawberry and more), as well as edible seeds, hazelnuts, wild onions, wild carrots, cattail reeds and soaproot.[20]

Among the most important tools for collecting, storing and preparing food were baskets, and basket making was also a woman's job. Very few examples of traditional Ohlone basketry remain, and the particular patterns and techniques used by Ohlone basket makers were lost by the middle of the twentieth century. Only in the first two decades of the twenty-first century, after careful study of surviving baskets and exhaustive research into their cultural context, was an Ohlone artist—Linda Yamane, of the Rumsien tribe of the Monterey area—able to recapture Ohlone basketry techniques.[21] Tule reeds, plentiful in the wetlands at the Valley's western end, were very common materials, as were willow sticks, sedge and rushes and big leaf maple. Work basketry included vessels for collecting and storing food, watertight vessels for carrying water and cooking, cradles and baby carriers; women also wove baskets for ceremonial purposes.

Men's work revolved around hunting and fishing and included the manufacture of bows, arrows, darts and atlatls, nets, decoys and traps.[22] Bows and arrows they used primarily for hunting larger game such as deer and elk. Individual hunters disguised their shape and scent, stalked an animal until they came close enough for a good shot and then trailed the wounded target until it died. Smaller game such as jackrabbits or quail might be driven in large groups into nets, caught in traps or speared with atlatl-launched darts. They caught fish in traps made of willow branches, with hook, line, sinker and bob, or stunned them with a mild toxin made from soaproot. To catch ducks and geese, Ohlone hunters used decoys to lure the birds down to the surface of a pond or marsh and then captured them with nets.

Warfare was also the realm of men. The most common causes of war between tribes seem to have been territorial disputes and the kidnapping of women. Men went to war with bow and arrow, ambushing enemy warriors and occasionally facing off in skirmishes of several warriors to a side. It is not entirely clear how the Ohlones ended these conflicts, although the frequency of intertribal marriage indicates that it played an important role in diplomacy and peacemaking.[23]

Trade served as the third leg of relations between tribes. Seasonal dances—at which neighboring tribes regularly gathered to socialize, perform ceremonial dances and exchange trade goods—were supplemented by irregular feasts, at which tribes enjoying an unusually good harvest invited their neighbors to share the bounty. The guest tribes at these feasts usually reciprocated with gifts of trade beads.[24]

The material and social facts of Ohlone life were underpinned by a view of the world in which supernatural forces and spiritual power held great, even determining, influence over everything. Maintaining a proper relationship with the powers of the world was of utmost importance, and rituals provided the tools for doing so.[25]

The most significant community rituals involved dances. Most of these were associated with the annual cycle of festivals; these probably included the Kuksu world-renewal ceremonies, which had spread to the Bay Area from northern groups such as the Pomos and Maidus and which many Ohlone and Miwok tribes seem to have practiced.[26] Other dances accompanied rituals for healing or rites of passage. Unfortunately, the details of dance traditions among the tribes of the Valley were not documented before the tribes had joined the missions.[27]

The lore that made sense of the tribe's rituals and lifeways was often framed in stories about the First People, mythic-age heroes identified with particular animals. Tales about Coyote or Kaknú the peregrine falcon (or any of the other First People in Ohlone stories) highlighted the tribe's connection to its home territory and often emphasized the negative consequences of greed or rule breaking.[28]

When the Spanish reached the Bay Area in the mid-eighteenth century, the Ohlone tribes of the Amador-Livermore Valley were part of a well-established human network, pursuing a way of life that had been largely stable for hundreds of years. Although it was not immediately apparent, the new arrivals posed a deadly threat to their society.

Before Pleasanton

The Mission Era, 1769–1834

After flirting with the idea of establishing a way station for the Manila galleons on the Northern California coast in the early seventeenth century, the Spanish Crown shelved any notion of colonizing the region for over a hundred years.[29] By the mid-eighteenth century, however, Russian fur traders had pushed too far south for Madrid's comfort, and the British had also begun to take an interest in the Pacific Northwest. Yet little money and manpower were available for so intensive an undertaking as colonizing Upper California. Therefore, the Spanish government adopted an approach that promised a highly efficient use of human and material resources: converting the natives to Christianity and gaining their loyalty to Spain in the process. The Franciscan Order, already administering the missions of Baja California after the dissolution of the Society of Jesus, was recruited to establish a chain of missions up the California coast, with the support of a small force of Spanish soldiers and an even smaller group of skilled artisans and their families.[30]

The advanced base for colonizing Northern California was Monterey, where a presidio and mission were built in 1770. Monterey served as a starting point for further exploration of Northern California, building on the knowledge gained in Gaspar de Portolà's initial expedition of 1769. The first of these forays to reach the Amador-Livermore Valley was the party of Pedro Fages and Father Juan Crespi, which passed through while returning south from the shores of the Carquinez Strait in 1772. The party passed down the western side of the Valley, entering from the San Ramon Valley late in the day on April 1:

> *Wednesday, April 1.—We set out at six, following the same valley* [San Ramon] *in a southerly direction, the excellence of the road continuing, with many trees. This day we covered ten leagues, all by the same valley, all level land, covered with grass and trees, with many and good arroyos, and with numerous villages of very gentle and peaceful heathen, many of them of fair complexion. It is a very suitable place for a good mission, having good lands, much water, firewood and many heathen. We stopped, after traveling ten leagues, in the same valley, on the bank of a running arroyo with plenty of water. At the entrance the valley has a width of a quarter of a league, and little by little it goes on widening up to four full leagues, which is probably also the width at this place.*

Thursday, April 2.—*We set out at six in the morning, still following the valley in a southerly direction. It continues with the same width until it gradually narrows. It is evident that the land is not so good now, and it is broken by some descents and small ravines, but it all continues full of oaks and live oaks, as does also the arroyo, which flows through the valley with an abundance of water and trees. In a league and a half of travel after our departure we crossed the arroyo, which had a good deal of water and a width of about six varras. As soon as this is passed the valley widens, making a valley three-quarters of a league wide with good land well forested with trees, like the one mentioned above. On the other side of the valley we crossed another arroyo even larger, also full of trees. In the southeastern part of this valley the two arroyos unite, and from the junction a good-sized river now flows in the same direction. The place is very desirable for a good mission, although we did not stop there I named it Santa Coleta.*[31]

Colonization and Conversion

Both Crown policy and Franciscan doctrine discouraged forced conversion; secular and religious authorities agreed that it was more likely to spark violent resistance. Spain could afford too few soldiers for this project to cope with organized resistance, and the Franciscans believed it important that Indians be baptized willingly—at least by a certain definition of "willingly," as we shall see; nonetheless, conversion at musket point was against official policy.[32]

The campaign to win hearts and minds, however, was to be conducted on Spanish terms more than Indian terms. Both officers and padres were liberal with gifts but also made it clear that the colonists would use force to defend what they considered theirs.[33] Even as the livestock they brought to California crowded out the game that Ohlones and Miwoks hunted, the Spanish inflicted swift punishment on Indians who stole or slew cattle and horses. European-style agriculture, with irrigation and plowing, also altered the delicate balance on which the native economy depended, and the Spanish further forbade the controlled burning that encouraged the growth of traditional food plants.[34] Most significantly, the padres regarded those who joined the missions as legal wards of the Franciscan Order, subject to close control over their everyday lives until they could demonstrate themselves fully converted *gente de razon* ("people of reason")—a goal they could not reach without giving up virtually all of their traditional culture.

The Franciscan program, in its ideal form, separated the new converts (or neophytes) from Indian society and resettled them within the mission walls.[35] Here they learned not only the elements of the Catholic faith but also skills that the padres believed they would need to become productive Spanish subjects: agriculture, animal husbandry, European-style crafts and industry. Frequent catechism and religious services impressed the religious message on the mission's neophytes. Catholic sexual morality, much stricter than that within tribal society, was enforced. Marriage by Christian rite was encouraged, and between couples already cohabiting it was mandatory. Unmarried women were locked in a dormitory (*monjerio*) every night, and their contact with men was carefully restricted. The padres required obedience in all matters and used floggings and public shaming to punish transgressions, sometimes even minor ones. Neophytes who tried to escape could expect to be retrieved by soldiers or by other neophytes, using force if necessary.

Indians who joined the mission understandably found it difficult to adjust to this new life and to the expectations of the Franciscan fathers. In addition to the conditions purposefully created by the missionaries, the mission environment proved hazardous to Indians' health. Dormitories were poorly ventilated; sanitation was not entirely adequate, and like many Native Americans, the Bay Area tribes lacked immunity to several diseases endemic in Europe. Measles and syphilis proved especially destructive.[36]

At the presidios and pueblos, the Spanish maintained trade relations with unbaptized ("gentile") tribes, hiring them as casual labor in exchange for trade goods. The Franciscans preferred not to let mission Indians work at the pueblos and presidios because they saw the soldiers and civilians as a sinful influence on their charges.[37] Both secular and religious authorities made an effort to prevent horses and European arms from circulating among the tribes, although the need for herdsmen eventually forced the Spanish to train Indian workers in horsemanship.

The early 1790s saw a significant upswing in baptisms for the Bay Area missions, as many tribes facing the destruction of their traditional means of subsistence joined the missions en masse despite the known threats to health and liberty they posed.[38] Although a number of individuals withdrew beyond Spain's reach and sought sanctuary with gentile tribes

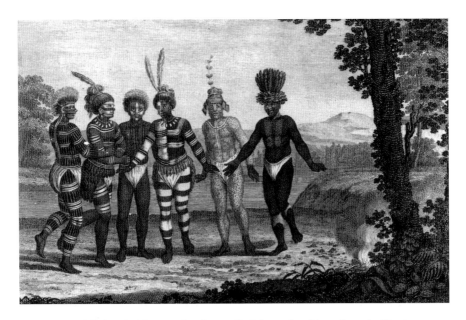

Neophytes at Mission San Jose performing a tribal dance for visitors from the Russian expedition headed by Nikolai Rezanov in 1806. *Bancroft Library.*

of the interior, it seems that more opted to join the missions. As noted, the mission economy thoroughly undermined the bases on which the native economy rested. Because neighboring tribes were interdependent, disrupting even a few tribes' means of subsistence had ripple effects that damaged the entire network of alliances and trade relationships. The spread of syphilis among gentile tribes in contact with the presidios and pueblos, as well as (perhaps even more than) among the neophytes of the missions, had become an epidemic. The ecological and demographic damage wrought by colonization threatened traditional society with complete collapse.

Joining in large groups also had its own advantages, at least over joining individually. It would be easier to maintain existing family and social ties. The missions were not equipped to handle so many residents and began allowing more neophytes to live off the mission grounds, away from direct supervision. Even within the missions, it was possible to maintain traditions in secret while remaining outwardly obedient, as supervision was so thinly spread.[39]

Establishing Mission San Jose

At this time, plans to expand the mission system moved forward, and in 1795, a party led by Lieutenant Hermenegildo Sal and Padre Antonio Danti went out to select the site for a mission to be established northeast of Mission Santa Clara, for the conversion of the tribes east of the hills and beyond.[40] Although there were a number of suitable locations in the Amador-Livermore Valley, the party decided on a site in present-day Fremont, on the hither side of the passes through the hills and just thirteen miles away from Mission Santa Clara; recent conflict with the Saclan tribe, who lived in the area around modern Lafayette, had made security a more significant concern. As a result, the Spanish exercised their claims over the Valley from the other side of Mission Pass, a decision that would protect the mission but expose its herds to raids by hostile tribes of the Central Valley.

Although baptisms dwindled to a trickle between 1795 and 1800, many of those who did convert came from the tribes of the Tri-Valley area.[41] Between 1800 and 1805, on the other hand, most of the tribes of the Amador, Livermore and San Ramon Valleys joined either Mission San Jose or Mission Santa Clara. Only the Luechas, whose lands lay southeast of the Livermore Valley, held out; in 1804, they attacked a mission party that had accidentally or intentionally come uninvited into their territory, and over the following year, a series of mutual reprisals led to their eventual submission and entry into Missions Santa Clara and San Jose by the end of 1806.[42]

The suppression of the Luechas left the Valley under Spanish control, but the herds and Christian villages subject to Mission San Jose still lay exposed to raiding by tribes from the Central Valley. After 1810, such raids became more frequent and more difficult to deal with.[43] Despite the Spaniards' efforts to prevent it, gentile tribes had acquired horses and learned to ride them. The Altamont Pass provided a direct route across the Central Coast range to the mission's herds in the Valley, as well as an equally direct route back to the Central Valley for Spanish reprisals. One of these reprisals, launched in 1819, included a young soldier named Agustin Bernal, who would later become one of the Valley's most prominent landowners.[44]

At the same time, the Franciscans frequently sent evangelizing parties into the Central Valley to recruit converts among the Yokuts-speaking tribes of the interior. Disease and low birth rates among the neophytes—not to mention runaways—resulted in a net loss of population that could only be countered by recruiting.[45] Furthermore, political turmoil in Spain and Mexico had cut California off from its usual supply sources, and the products of the missions became increasingly vital to the survival of the colony. Their beef and other agricultural products fed not only neophytes and missionaries but also the soldiers of the presidios and the civilians of the pueblos. The manufactures of neophyte artisans provided tools, clothing and furniture, and the herds also produced the hides and tallow that served as California's primary exports to the Russian and British traders who supplied what the colony could not make for itself.

The End of the Missions

As the 1810s turned into the 1820s, however, significant changes loomed on the horizon for California and for the mission system in particular. After years of civil war, Mexico turned a declaration of independence into a fact in 1821. The new government was republican, not particularly friendly to the Franciscans and ready to begin the project of secularizing mission lands.

When the Spanish government authorized the mission project, its long-term goal was to turn the mission lands over to the Indians once they had been suitably converted and assimilated, converting the missions themselves into parish churches. But politics pushed the future of the mission lands in an entirely different direction. To begin with, the padres were reluctant to declare their charges ready for integration into the society of the pueblos and presidios. They protested (with reason) that the mission Indians had not completely let go of their old traditions; they also feared that the sinful ways of the pueblos and presidios would be a bad influence on these new subjects of Spain.[46] And although they never said so, they may also have feared losing control over Indian labor and the wealth that it generated. They resisted attempts to declare the Indians *gente de razon*, spiritually and culturally "of age" and ready to participate as adults in California society.

In addition, many lay settlers (both military and civilian) had developed ambitions of their own. For nearly half a century, they had also struggled to build this colony, and many saw the potential breakup of mission lands as an opportunity to become the sort of landed gentry that occupied the upper tiers of society back in Spain. Provincial governors had been empowered to make private grants nearly since the founding of California; the earliest *ranchos* were established in the 1780s on land lying outside the boundaries of the missions, presidios and pueblos. But the missions held large areas of some of the best land in Spanish California, and there were many *Californios* still looking for the opportunity to acquire a piece of grazing land—ideally, with a ready source of Indian labor to work it.

The struggles over secularization were drawn out over some twenty years, dating from the official secularization order issued by Madrid in 1813.[47] Political instability in Mexico, both during and after the Revolution, helped prevent any higher authority from imposing a solution on the opposing sides in California. An experimental plan to emancipate selected neophyte families, introduced in 1826 by Governor José Maria Echeandia, failed when few of the Indians (who had few other opportunities) chose to leave the missions.[48] Eight years later, a new governor, José Figueroa, drew up a plan with input from colonial representatives. The missions would be secularized in three groups between 1834 and 1836. The missions themselves would become towns, and their churches would be handed over to parish priests. Part of the lands and half of the herds would be distributed to neophytes, who would also be liable to work on the undistributed mission lands until they were granted as ranchos.[49] Mission San Jose fell into the first group, and José de Jesus Vallejo was appointed its administrator in the fall of 1834.

Ranchos and Ranchers, 1834–1862

Dissolving Mission San Jose

The administrator appointed to oversee the secularization of Mission San Jose was José de Jesus Vallejo, an experienced soldier and the elder brother of the more famous Mariano Vallejo.[50] Vallejo began work at the end of 1836, taking inventory of mission assets and tracking the various— and sometimes conflicting—orders for loans, sales and grants that passed through his hands. Governor Figueroa had hoped to protect the Indians' rights to mission land and livestock, but he lacked the manpower to enforce a policy unpopular among the colonists; his successors did

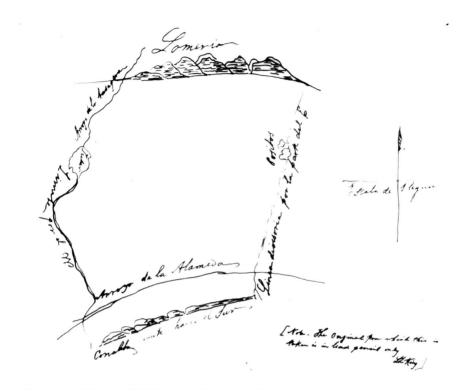

Diseño map of Rancho El Valle de San Jose, circa 1838. *Museum on Main.*

not even try. As well-connected Californios jockeyed for access to the missions' best lands and livestock, the former neophytes largely opted out of the system. Some left to join the tribes of the interior; others moved to towns or ranchos and became casual laborers. Very few were willing to continue working on other peoples' land as the condition for having a plot of their own.[51]

The first grant of Mission San Jose lands in the Valley actually preceded Vallejo's appointment. José Maria Amador, who had served as *mayordomo* (ranch foreman) for Mission San Jose from 1827 to 1835, received five square leagues (more than twenty thousand acres) of land in 1834.[52] Amador's grant, named Rancho San Ramón, covered the northern part of the Amador-Livermore Valley, around present-day Dublin, and extended north into the San Ramon Valley, which was named after the rancho. Applications by others soon followed, and over the next four years, these submissions reached the governor's office, were tabled, weighed against one another and became the subject of various lobbying efforts until in 1839 three more patents divided up the remaining lands of the Amador-Livermore Valley.

Farthest east lay Rancho Las Positas, about twenty thousand acres, granted to José Noriega and English immigrant Robert Livermore, who had been pasturing herds on the land since 1834.[53] Just south of Rancho San Ramón lay the nearly nine thousand acres of Rancho Santa Rita, granted to José Dolores Pacheco; part of this grant would later be annexed to Pleasanton. The southernmost, and largest, grant consisted of more than forty-eight thousand acres in the southwestern portion of the Valley; it was named Rancho Valle de San José, and the grantees were two brothers and their two brothers-in-law: Agustin and Juan Pablo Bernal, Antonio Maria Pico (husband of Maria Pilar Bernal) and Antonio Maria Suñol (husband of Maria Dolores Bernal). All four were prominent members of the Californio community centered in Pueblo de San José. Pico had been *alcalde* (chief magistrate and administrator) of the town and Suñol a highly successful merchant. The Bernal brothers were sons of the veteran soldier José Joaquin Bernal, who had settled in the Santa Clara Valley after retirement and received a patent in 1835 for the lands he had developed under the title Rancho Santa Teresa.

Agustin and Juan Pablo Bernal

Baptized in San Francisco on August 28, 1797, Agustin Bernal was the fourth child of José Joaquin Bernal and Maria Josefa Sanchez, both of whom arrived in California with the De Anza Expedition of 1776 and were married at the San Francisco presidio in 1785. In 1807, the family moved to Pueblo de San José, where Agustin grew up. He enlisted in the army in 1819, enrolling in the Company of San Francisco and serving both at the presidio and at Mission San Jose, where raiding by tribes from across the Central Coast range had become a serious concern. During his military tour, he more than once had occasion to travel through the Amador-Livermore Valley.

Agustin's first wife was Josefa Antonia Gregoria Berreyessa; although the date of the wedding is not currently known, their first child was born in 1823. Agustin remained with the San Francisco Company for four more years and then resigned his position to move to the city of San Jose, near the lands where his father had settled. He lived at the pueblo until his father's

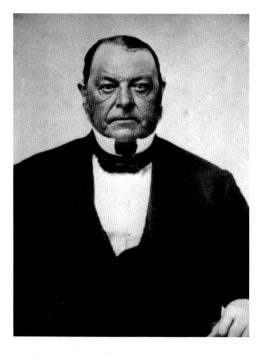

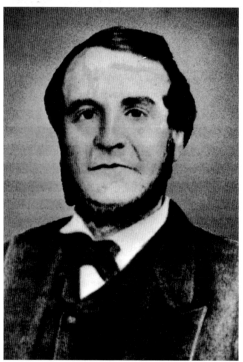

death in 1837, whereupon he moved to Rancho Santa Teresa; Josefa Antonia died in childbirth two years later. In 1841, he married again; his new bride was Maria Juana Higuera, a girl of a prominent family some twenty-seven years his junior.[54]

Juan Pablo Bernal was born in 1810, nearly thirteen years after Agustin, and was the eleventh of twelve children. Unlike Agustin, he did not join the military and seems to have spent his youth in preparation for the life of a *ranchero*: riding, hunting, tending livestock and so forth. He was married in 1832 to Rafaela Feliz, also the daughter of colonists. The couple soon moved to Rancho Santa Teresa, where they lived with his parents and several of his siblings' families. Around 1840, the couple moved to San Jose, building a home on Market Square, the pueblo's central plaza.

Top: Agustin Bernal, circa 1860. *Museum on Main.*

Left: Portrait of Juan Pablo Bernal, date unknown. *Museum on Main.*

Both Agustin and Juan Pablo kept their residences in the Santa Clara Valley for the first decade after securing Rancho Valle de San José—Agustin on Rancho Santa Teresa, helping his mother look after the estate, and Juan Pablo in San Jose. Direct management of the rancho's lands and herds they entrusted to a hired mayordomo and the vaqueros working under him. The first of these was Francisco Alviso, nephew of José Maria Amador; Alviso stayed two years before leaving to work for his uncle at Rancho San Ramón.[55]

Rancho Life

The rancho lifestyle has been romanticized in popular memory as an endless cycle of fandangos and feasts, punctuated by the occasional cattle roundup.[56] There is some truth to this picture. The rancheros controlled most of California's wealth and political power; because they could rely on cheap, mostly Indian labor, they rarely had to trouble themselves with the physically taxing or dangerous aspects of their livelihoods. There was little formal education—Juan Pablo Bernal, for instance, never learned his letters and was not considered unusual for it. Yet on the whole they took the responsibilities of patronage and hospitality seriously; graciousness and munificence were highly regarded among the ranchero class. Although immigration and natural increase had lifted California's population, human resources were still valuable enough that Mexico encouraged immigration to the province, and rancheros had incentive to treat their dependents well. Within the family—although a patriarch had the authority to lock up his daughters for the better protection of their virtue, to arrange marriages for his children and even to make major decisions for them after marriage—the mores of his class obliged him to exercise his power with respect and consideration, although they also demanded that children display deference and obedience to their parents. Legal traditions enshrined property rights for women and provided recourse against abusive husbands. The limited number of ranchero families and the high degree of intermarriage among them also meant that most rancheros had family ties with one another.

Although the ranchos raised sheep for wool and horses for riding and engaged in some agriculture on the side, their major export products were hides and tallow from the vast herds of cattle.[57] News of the trading ships' arrival brought massive drives of cattle to places near the coast.

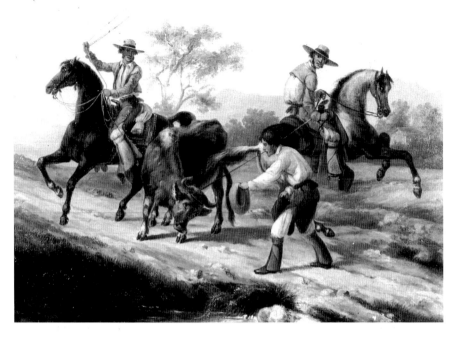

Vaqueros roping a steer. Painting by Augusto Ferran, circa 1849. *Bancroft Library.*

The *rodeo* (roundup) was a big social event, accompanied by music, dancing and feasting. When the cattle reached their destination, the *matanza* (slaughter) began; vaqueros and sailors joined forces to slaughter, skin and render them as quickly as possible. The hides, which came to be known as "California banknotes," were stretched out to dry, while the rendered fat was collected in bags, to prepare both products for shipping. Beef not eaten during the matanza was dried for jerky, and the carcasses were left behind for wild animals to finish off.

Secularization had not deterred the tribes of the Central Valley from raiding the settlers' horses and cattle, and the Amador-Livermore Valley remained a convenient target. Juan Pablo Bernal later recalled an incident in April 1848 in which a party of sixteen men—including himself, Robert Livermore and Antonio Maria Pico—tracked a raiding party back across the mountains to retrieve a string of more than 150 horses; in the ensuing confrontation, the rancheros' party killed eight of the nine Indians, suffered two wounded and brought nearly all of the horses back home.[58]

The American Conquest

By 1848, California had become a territory of the United States, ceded by Mexico in the Treaty of Guadalupe Hidalgo after a two-year war fought more south of the Rio Grande than in California. The United States' interest in California dated back to the 1820s but had increased considerably by 1845 as land-hungry homesteaders pushed westward.[59] Attempts to purchase the province from Mexico had been fruitless, but the U.S. annexation of the Republic of Texas—and inheritance of its simmering boundary dispute with Mexico—provided the spark for a war of conquest. While U.S. and Mexican troops glared at one another across the disputed Texas boundary, Captain John C. Frémont of the U.S. Army Corps of Topographical Engineers exceeded his instructions and led a mapping expedition across the Sierra Nevada Mountains into California. Frémont passed through the Amador-Livermore Valley on his way to Monterey, noting a stay with Antonio Suñol in his memoirs.[60] (The horses he is said to have requisitioned from the ranchos go unmentioned.[61]) Urged to leave by local authorities, he nonetheless ended up supporting an uprising in Sonoma instigated by mostly American settlers, who declared a "California Republic" without knowing that the United States had recently declared war.[62] Supporting U.S. forces arrived at Monterey in July, and the forces of the Bear Flag Republic were absorbed into those of the United States.

The Mexican response was complicated by unstable provincial politics; the military commander in the north was on the verge of armed conflict with the provincial governor in Los Angeles, and even though the two were willing to make common cause against the Yankees, General Castro could not recruit enough militia in the Bay Area to make a stand without giving up the region.[63] Juan Pablo Bernal was one of those who joined; it is not clear how much action he might have seen, but he seems to have escaped without serious injury.[64] Agustin, nearly fifty at the outbreak of hostilities, remained at home rather than put on his old uniform to fight.[65]

The treaty that signed California and New Mexico over to the United States specified that land grants made under Spanish and Mexican rule would be respected, a provision that in theory should have left the rancheros with no cause for concern about their properties. However, landowners would have to prove the titles of their holdings—and, more challenging, the boundaries of the same—to a commission appointed by the federal government.⁶⁶ In addition, the vast ranchos had begun to attract squatters from among the immigrant population, a problem that would be greatly exacerbated after the discovery of gold in central California inspired a new and immense wave of immigration.

Preserving Rancho Valle de San José

Fortunately, the owners of Rancho Valle de San José found a valuable ally among the new wave of immigrants: John W. Kottinger. Kottinger was born in Moravia, a province of the Austrian Empire, in 1820. As a youth, he attended the prestigious *Academisches Gymnasium* in Vienna and then the University of Olomouc, earning his teaching certificate in 1841.⁶⁷ After a few years spent tutoring children of the Habsburg Monarchy's elites, in 1846 Kottinger immigrated to the United States. He landed in New Orleans and made his way to Kentucky, where he was associated with newspaper publisher George D. Prentice, known for his support of the nativist, anti-Catholic Know-Nothing movement.⁶⁸ In 1847, Kottinger left for Brazil, where he spent a year or two before heading for California, via Chile, in 1849. He arrived in San Francisco on September 16.

But Kottinger was not meant for the gold fields. After a short time in San Francisco, he relocated to San Jose, where he opened a school and acted as an interpreter in the courts of Santa Clara County. In San Jose, he also encountered the Bernals, and in 1850, he married Juan Pablo Bernal's second daughter, Maria Refugia Bernal y Feliz. In 1851, he was commissioned a notary public and admitted to the California bar.⁶⁹

Having a son-in-law in the legal profession was very convenient for Juan Pablo—and for the Bernal family in general. As noted previously, the titles and boundaries of properties guaranteed by the Treaty of Guadalupe Hidalgo had to be confirmed to the satisfaction of the American legal system. And the *diseños* and descriptions that established the ranchos' boundaries under Mexican law were anything but satisfactory by U.S. standards. Because the ranchos were primarily free-range cattle operations, their precise boundaries were less important to their owners (and to the authorities) than the ability to properly identify which cattle belonged to whom. As a result, Mexican land grants and the diseños that mapped them were distressingly vague by a standard established to define precise property lines in country where farm plots abutted right up against one another.

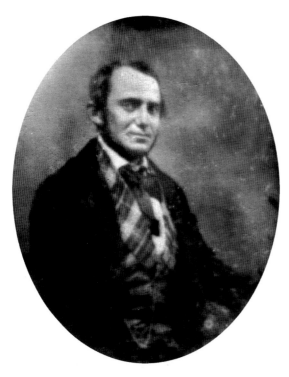

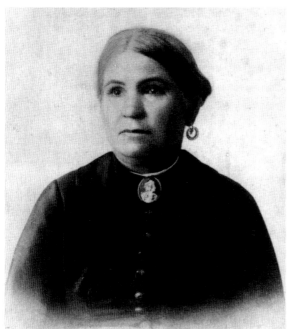

Top: John W. Kottinger, circa 1850. *Museum on Main.*

Left: Maria Refugia Bernal y Kottinger, circa 1860. *Museum on Main.*

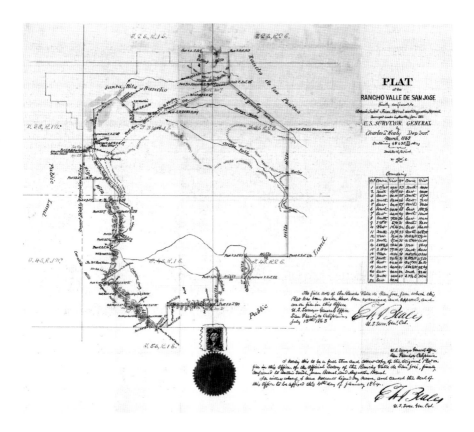

With Kottinger's assistance, the Bernals were able to get title to Rancho Valle de San José confirmed in January 1854; confirming its boundaries, however, would require another nine years.[70] In the meantime, the map of the Valley was already changing, as the Bernals' neighbors had begun to sell their claims rather than drag them through the confirmation process. José Dolores Pacheco sold half of Rancho Santa Rita to his mayordomo Francisco Alviso in 1851, and after Pacheco's death in 1852, his heirs sold the rest.[71] José Maria Amador sold ten thousand acres from the southern half of Rancho San Ramón to James W. Dougherty in 1852. Robert Livermore bought out his partner, José Noriega, in an 1854 land swap to strengthen his holdings. Antonio Pico had already sold his share of El Valle in 1842 to Antonio Suñol, who sold it to Juan Pablo Bernal in 1849, leaving Juan Pablo owner of half of the rancho. Suñol held on to his original share, passing it to his heirs upon his death in 1865.[72]

In 1851, even before title to Rancho El Valle had been confirmed, Kottinger convinced Juan Pablo to divide up his share of the property by distributing

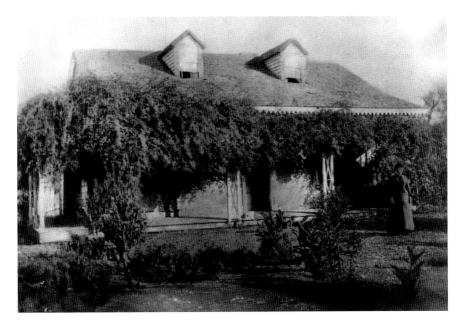

Above: The Kottinger Adobe in the late nineteenth century. The building was torn down in 1930. *Museum on Main.*

Opposite: Plat map of Rancho El Valle de San Jose, 1863. *Museum on Main.*

portions to his wife and six children, the apparent idea being to protect the family assets against threatened lawsuits.[73] In practice, the settlement allowed the younger Bernal generation—in particular Refugia and her husband—to sell acreage without obtaining the patriarch's permission; it also complicated the surveying when Agustin later sued for an equitable distribution of the rancho's lands among its various claimants.

At the same time, both Bernal brothers decided that it would be in their best interests to relocate from the Santa Clara Valley to Rancho El Valle. There were plenty of family members to look after Rancho Santa Teresa during its own confirmation process, but none of the family had established residency on the larger grant. In addition, by 1849, many would-be prospectors were crossing the Amador-Livermore Valley on their way to the gold fields, each one potentially a squatter or a livestock thief. Agustin had already begun constructing an adobe near the western foothills in 1848, and he moved his immediate family there in 1850.[74] The Kottingers soon followed, moving into an adobe house south of the

Arroyo de Valle in 1851, and the following year, Juan Pablo settled into an adobe on the opposite bank of the arroyo from the Kottingers.[75] The vicinity of the three Bernal family adobes became known as the Alisal, after a local grove of sycamore trees, and in the gold rush era, it would earn a reputation as a rough neighborhood.

The Gold Rush: Beef and Bandits

In spite of its risks, the California Gold Rush created great opportunities for the rancheros of the Amador-Livermore Valley, mostly because the camps created a large and ready market for beef on the hoof. Livermore, Amador and the Bernals earned a lot of money driving their cattle into the gold country for sale.[76] Unfortunately, the occasional stolen cow or squatter's shack was not the only danger of the gold rush era. The influx of newcomers helped further destabilize a society already shaken by the conquest, and crime rose accordingly.

Bandit stories of the gold rush era are as plentiful as they are hard to verify, and tales of the Amador-Livermore Valley are harder to verify than most; in the early 1850s, the region was thinly populated, lacked regular news coverage and lay many miles from the nearest centers of law and order in San Jose and Oakland. The Valley also bordered Niles Canyon, where the most notorious bandit in California's history is supposed to have had a small homestead. Because of all these factors, stories about Joaquin Murrieta figure largely in the lore of the period.

According to Kottinger family tradition, Murrieta actually worked for the Bernals before embarking on a life of crime and afterward paid the occasional "visit" to demand bread or other supplies. One of the more exciting incidents has become embedded in family lore:

> *It was the custom to take the gold either to San Jose or San Francisco and make a deposit with Wells Fargo. Juan Pablo and his son-in-law had set out early in the morning for San Francisco and Rafaela* [Juan Pablo's wife] *had remained at the Kottinger adobe with her daughter. About two hours after the departure of Juan Pablo and Kottinger, Murieta* [sic] *rode into the yard and seeing Rafaela at the window sewing, he fired a shot which hit a silver thimble on the sill and lodged in the wall beyond. Rafaela was thoroughly startled and Refugia, hearing the commotion, came to the front yard. When she*

saw the bandits, she invited them into the house to eat. A great meal was served to Joaquin and his men, taking so much time that Juan Pablo and John Kottinger were far away and beyond pursuit when Joaquin politely took his leave of the ladies and the lives and gold of the two prominent pioneers were saved.[77]

A different encounter with Murrieta's band was published in the *Pleasanton Times* in January 1891, nearly forty years after Murrieta's highly publicized (though frequently disputed) death in July 1853. The "Claudio" who stars as the lead villain in this story would have been Murrieta's brother-in-law, Claudio Feliz, who was killed by a posse near Salinas in the fall of 1852:

Joaquin Murrietta's [sic] band were quite numerous and somewhat scattered about when they found it most expedient. Joaquin himself, in disguise had partaken of the hospitality of the place. Mr. Kottinger was the next victim selected by them (undoubtedly for the energy displayed in bringing offenders to justice) to kill and rob. So Claudio, one of Joaquin's most trusted lieutenants and six others were dispatched for the purpose. They arrived by way of San Jose, Sept. 27th, and tethered their horses in the creek. Three of the men cautiously advanced towards the house; they accosted Mr. Kottinger (not knowing him, as he had just returned home covered with dust) the leader asking him if the padrona was in, the reply was "yes." The men entered the house without knocking and demanded some bread. Mr. Kottinger had worked his way in and sat partially in the shadow of the outer door. It was past twilight; the forward man, Claudio, made a move as though he would pay for the bread, putting his hand in his breast pocket, and as he did so Mrs. Kottinger saw the gleam of a poniard as it was being drawn out, and screaming at the same time flew out of the room. Mr. Kottinger was not asleep while all this was going on. Taking in the situation at a glance, he noticed the men, at least two of them, were near the outside door, the one they came in; he instantly, with superhuman effort, thrust them outside and barred the door. All of this was done much quicker than pen could write; the women had closed the other outside door. The robbers had noticed that there was a bedroom window open; to this window they rushed. Almost at the same time the family thought of this weak point of their castle; Mr. Kottinger, terrified at the possibility of the villains gaining admission, ran to the window. He was none too soon. Four men were clambering up and over the window sill. Frenzied at the sight of the men, he boldly swung the shutter in their faces with a tremendous effort; at the same time came the crash of bullets through the frail protector around him. Another round was given, and the retreat was made. A party in pursuit of these men heard the noise, but the rascals had fled. Three days afterwards six of their number were killed, including Claudio.[78]

The *Times'* editors included this anecdote as part of an article on the fiftieth anniversary of the Kottinger adobe's construction. For some reason, they dated the incident to 1862, years after both Feliz and Murrieta were dead. The story was unsourced, although in 1891, Kottinger lived in nearby San Jose (where he would die the following year) and still had children residing in the Pleasanton area, any one of whom might have supplied the tale to the newspaper.[79] Even in 1852, assuming the date to be in error, the incident as described would have been unlikely, although it could have been inspired by an encounter with other, less notorious outlaws.

Local Government in an Era of Transition

The advent of statehood brought with it a redrafting of California's political map, to bring it more into conformity with the United States' conventions of government. The first version adopted divided the eastern shore of the Bay and its hinterland between Contra Costa and Santa Clara Counties, with the Amador-Livermore Valley included in Contra Costa. The affiliation did not last long, however; at the request of Alameda and Santa Clara Counties, in 1853 the legislature combined the northernmost township of Santa Clara County (Washington) with approximately the southern half of Contra Costa County to form Alameda County.[80] The new county government subdivided Alameda into six townships, reduced to five by the end of the year. The largest and most thinly populated of these encompassed the entire Amador-Livermore and Sunol Valleys from the summit of the western hill line to the portion of the Coastal Range that marked Alameda County's eastern border. This region, covering nearly half of Alameda County's total area, was Murray Township.

It took more than a year for the county to expand its administrative structure to the level of the townships. The first elections in 1853 elected only county-wide officials (including several at-large justices and constables), as well as representatives to the state assembly and senate. In the fall of 1854, the townships elected their first constables and justices of the peace. In Murray Township, John W. Kottinger's legal experience made him a natural choice for the latter post; he was reelected annually until he relocated to San Francisco in 1858.[81]

Apart from its representative on the board of supervisors, Murray Township's formal government consisted entirely of its JPs and constables; everything else was handled at the county level.[82] Beginning in 1855, these numbered two each, meaning that two judges and two policemen represented law and order for nearly four hundred square miles of territory, thinly populated and with only the most basic of roads. To make matters worse, the county sheriff rarely took any interest in Murray Township until after Harry Morse began his second term in 1865. Kottinger is said to have done his best under these circumstances, dispensing justice from his home and holding prisoners in his adobe barn until they could be transferred to the county jail; local lore even holds that he excavated a tunnel between the two in order to transport prisoners safely from court to lockup.[83]

By the end of 1857, John W. Kottinger was clearly ready for a change. Perhaps he had grown tired of cattle ranching. Perhaps he found the lawlessness of the Valley too dangerous for his growing family. Perhaps he was simply sick of living in a backwater. Whatever the reason, Kottinger moved with Refugia and the children to San Francisco, leasing out their property on the rancho and taking up the real estate business.[84] The Kottingers' absence would only be temporary, however; four years later, they would return just as significant changes loomed over the Valley, and Kottinger would help usher in the new era by founding a town called Pleasanton.

PART II
PLEASANTON SMALL

A New Community: Unincorporated Pleasanton, 1862–1894

The 1860s presented the Valley with a dazzling opportunity for growth, as plans took shape to extend the transcontinental railroad through Murray Township. The railroad would need stops in the Valley to load its residents' products and unload their purchases, and existing towns would be preferable locations to build those stations. John W. Kottinger seized the moment and began to carve a town out of his family's share of Rancho Valle de San José as the railroad plans became known. This town, at or near the place called the Alisal, became Pleasanton, and for two decades after the railroad opened in 1869, it grew rapidly, creating a vibrant if small community unencumbered by municipal government yet increasingly aware of challenges that only incorporation might be able to tame.

The Coming of the Railroad

The first hints that a railway might be laid through the Valley came in June 1853, when a U.S. Army survey team under Lieutenant R.S. Williamson passed through while investigating potential routes linking San Francisco to the Central Valley.[85] The Williamson party came south from Benicia, over the road through the San Ramon Valley, and spent four days exploring and taking notes before moving on through the Altamont Pass into the Central Valley. At the end of the expedition, Williamson concluded that the Amador-Livermore Valley would provide one of the two easiest routes.

Concrete plans to build a line, however, did not crystallize until the end of 1862, when the Western Pacific Railroad (WP) was chartered. This company shared several directors with the San Francisco and San Jose Railroad, which was already under construction and would be completed in 1864.[86] The Western Pacific obtained the rights for the San Francisco–Sacramento line from the Central Pacific, planning to run a line from San Jose through Niles Canyon into the Amador-Livermore Valley and across through the Altamont Pass, from which it would turn north in the San Joaquin Valley and link up with the Central Pacific line near Sacramento. John Kottinger is likely to have known about this plan when he began selling plots for a town near the Alisal in 1863.

Construction on the San Jose–Sacramento line began in 1865, after completion of the San Francisco and San Jose. The Western Pacific managed to lay track from San Jose to Niles before financial difficulties forced a hiatus in October 1866. The Central Pacific's directors bought up the WP's rights, materials and rolling stock the following year, but they did not resume construction until the spring of 1869.[87] Although planners apparently at some point considered following the existing stagecoach route through Dougherty Station (the future Dublin), the final version took a more direct route through Pleasanton toward Livermore. This route had the further advantage of avoiding the "Bolsa" or "Laguna," the tule marsh that lay between Pleasanton and Dougherty Station. The new crews worked quickly, and by September the line was open for service.[88]

Establishing a Town

In 1862, the Kottingers returned to Rancho El Valle from their sojourn in San Francisco, and John W. Kottinger quickly put his newly earned real estate experience to work. In 1863, Kottinger sold three plots, totaling ten acres, from his and Maria Refugia's portion of the rancho lands, with the apparent intent of encouraging the growth of Alisal.[89] He had very

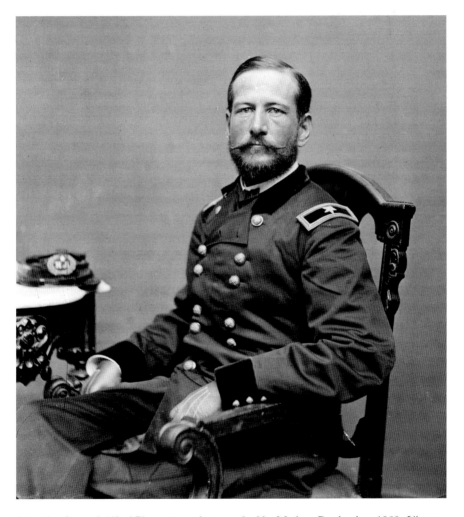

Brigadier General Alfred Pleasonton, photographed by Mathew Brady, circa 1862. *Library of Congress.*

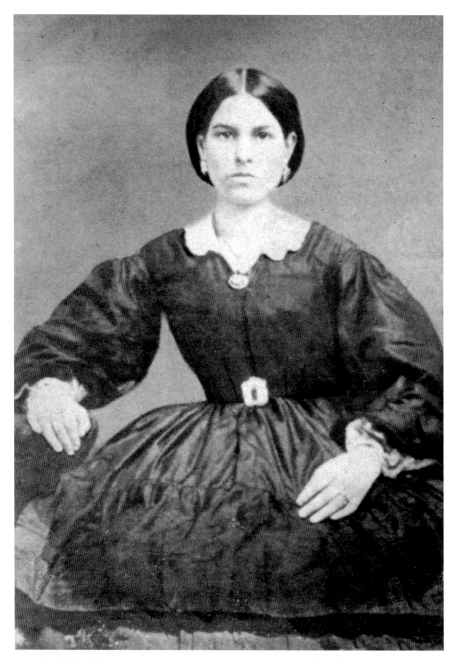

Angela Bernal Neal, circa 1865. Part of the land she brought into her marriage to Joshua Neal became the southeastern portion of Pleasanton's original layout. *Museum on Main.*

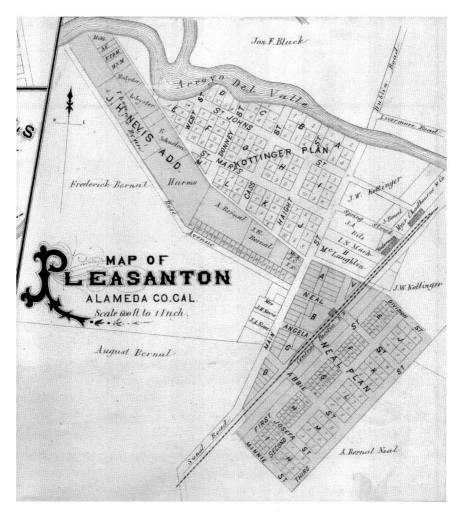

Map of Pleasanton in 1878, showing Kottinger's and Neal's original subdivisions, as well as what was established by Joseph Nevis after his marriage to Maria Higuera Bernal. *Thompson & West, Historical Atlas of Alameda County.*

likely heard about plans to build a railroad through the Valley that would connect San Jose with Sacramento, thus extending the transcontinental route all the way to San Francisco. By September 1864, the town was already being referred to as "Pleasanton"; on the ninth, the *Sacramento Daily Union*'s "Announcements" column mentioned a daughter born to Mrs. J.W. Kottinger at Pleasanton—a notice almost certainly submitted by Kottinger himself.[90]

Kottinger chose the name to honor General Alfred Pleasonton, a Union cavalry commander whose exploits had been well reported (and, according to later historians, rather embellished) in the West Coast press. The discrepancy in spelling, local tradition continues, was the responsibility of a postal clerk in Washington who took it upon himself to correct "Pleasonton" to "Pleasanton."[91] If the tale is true, the clerk was in good company: most California newspapers, both during and after the war, seem to have preferred the spelling "Pleasanton" when referring to the general.[92]

Kottinger found a partner for this town-founding enterprise in his neighbor Joshua Ayres Neal. A native of New Hampshire, Neal came to California in 1847 and had lived in the Valley since at least 1850, working as a ranch foreman for Robert Livermore.[93] By 1863, he had married Agustin Bernal's daughter Angela, and the two built a house not far south of the Kottinger adobe, near where Agustin's portion of the rancho met Juan Pablo's. Kottinger and Neal commissioned complementary surveys of adjoining portions of their lands, including the plots that Kottinger had already sold in the past few years. The products of these surveys were the first official maps of Pleasanton; they would, however, be corrected two years later to adjust for the railroad's final route.[94] The boundary between the Neal and Kottinger portions of the town plan was recognized under the name "Division Street," the name it still bears today.

Population: Growth and Change

The effect of the railroad on the development of the Valley was profound. Pleasanton and Livermore grew rapidly, eclipsing Dougherty Station as rail traffic on the new route dwarfed that on the old stage line. From 1860 to 1870, the population of the Valley ballooned from 514 to 2,400, but only 320 of Murray Township residents in 1870 lived in the district defined by the Dougherty Station Post Office, as opposed to 1,000 in Pleasanton's census district and 1,080 in Livermore's.[95]

This wave of immigration accelerated the growing Anglo domination of the Valley. In 1860, Californios made up more than 30 percent of Murray Township's population, another 10 percent had arrived from Mexico or Chile (some almost certainly before the gold rush) and about 4 percent the Census Bureau categorized as "Indians." Immigrants from Europe and Canada and migrants from other parts of the United

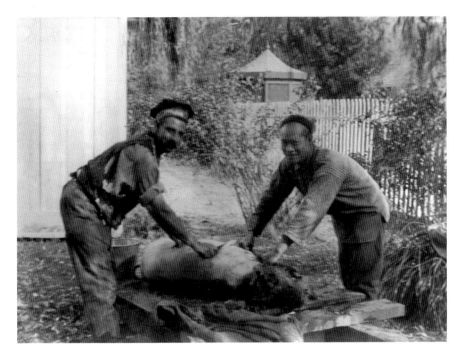

Two immigrant laborers skinning a pig on the Kottinger ranch in the 1870s or 1880s. The man on the left may be a Frenchman named Patain. The other man, identified as "Okeit," was one of Kottinger's many Chinese workers. *Museum on Main.*

States composed slightly more than half of the Valley's residents; the largest group of these belonged to Irish families who had come either directly or by way of the eastern United States, Canada or Australia. By 1870, Californios and Latin American immigrants constituted only about 10 percent of the Valley's population, whereas those from Europe or North America beyond the Sierras now represented about three-fourths of the total.

At the same time, however, the Valley's Native American population grew in proportion to that of Murray Township as a whole, thanks largely to the establishment of the Alisal Ranchería on Agustin Bernal's land. In addition, the Chinese population of the region rose more than a hundredfold, from 1 person in 1860 to 128 in 1870; many of these residents were listed as "railroad workers" by the census takers.

The European immigrants to the Valley included a significant number of Germans; names such as Duerr, Nusbaumer and Luders turn up in the 1860 and 1870 censuses. To the extent that these formed an ethnic community, its cultural center of gravity lay to the east in Livermore, a town founded in the eastern portion of the Rancho El Valle by William Mendenhall. The 1870s also saw the arrival of many Danish immigrants, and in later years, Danish families would become noted in the Valley for their role in the dairy industry.

About 30 Portuguese immigrants were living in Murray Township in 1870, including such prominent Pleasanton residents as farmer Joseph Nevis, hotelier Jason Rose and druggist Joseph Silver. Over the next decade, however, the size of the Valley's Portuguese community would increase by more than 1,000 percent, with more than 320 Portuguese immigrants and their children living in the Valley in 1880.[96] The vast majority of these immigrants came from the Azores Islands, a Portuguese dependency nearly a thousand miles off of the Iberian coast. In Pleasanton, the Azorean religious confraternity IDES (*Irmandades do Divino Espirito Santo*) would come to play a significant role in the town's social and cultural activities with its annual Holy Ghost Parade.

Although European immigrant groups were quickly accepted as part of the larger Pleasanton community—even the Portuguese, whose southern European origins and Catholic religion marked them for discrimination in other parts of the country—Chinese immigrants were subject to much of the same racism and social exclusion in the Valley that they faced in the rest of California. Letters to the local papers decried the employment of Chinese labor; the establishment of Chinese businesses, especially laundries, often generated protests in Livermore and Pleasanton. A local Anti-Coolie League was formed in 1886, four years after Congress passed a national Chinese Exclusion Act to restrict immigration, and although it is not clear that the organization remained particularly active afterward, both Pleasanton and Livermore sent delegates to anti-Chinese conventions in the following decades.[97]

The Breakup of the Ranchos

In 1866, a lawsuit filed by Agustin Bernal resulted in a thorough survey of Rancho Valle de San José and apportionment of its lands among its various claimants.[98] Taking into account the varying quality and value of the rancho's acreage, the referees attempted to distribute land equitably by value without straying too far from the boundaries established by earlier transfers. They began by dividing the rancho into three sections:

the northern and eastern representing the shares of Juan Pablo Bernal and Antonio Pico (the latter since purchased by Juan Pablo), the western representing Agustin's share and the southern comprising the portion of Antonio Suñol. Individual claims were assigned in the section of the grantee from whom title derived, often in non-adjacent plots so as to balance out the assignment of good and poor land.

At this time, most of the rancho's land was still owned by members of the grantees' families. Both Agustin and Juan Pablo had transferred considerable portions to their children and in-laws, while the estate of recently deceased Antonio Suñol still retained title to well over half of his original share. Out of Agustin's quarter-share, less than 14 percent of the land's value had been transferred out of the family. Juan Pablo's half-share was more heavily subdivided, but even so, nearly two-thirds of the property remained in his hands or those of his children and their spouses. These proportions would change considerably in the following years, as agriculture continued to crowd out stock raising and more Bernal descendants sold their property, often to cover debts.

Agricultural Transformation

The 1860s saw a gradual transition in the Valley's economy as grain farming overtook stock raising in significance, a transition capped by the completion of the railroad and its promise of easy market access. This transition may have received extra impetus from a severe drought in the middle of the decade, during which thousands of Valley sheep and cattle died from insufficient pasturage and drinking water. In 1860, census takers counted more than forty thousand sheep and nearly thirty-two thousand cattle on the farms of Murray Township but fewer than 8,000 bushels of grain, and only seven farmers out of the sixty-eight surveyed produced any significant quantities of grain.[99] By 1870, the western half alone produced nearly 300,000 bushels of wheat and more than 70,000 of barley; hay production rose less spectacularly, but in 1870, western Murray Township still produced nearly twice as much hay as the entire Valley had ten years before. The number of sheep and cattle seems to have dropped: the Pleasanton/Dublin area counted fewer than eight hundred cattle and a little more than seven thousand sheep in 1870, although the number of horses may actually have risen due to the larger number of farms and the importance of horses as work animals.[100]

By the end of the 1880s, grains had ceded pride of place to other crops, primarily wine grapes, hops and sugar beets. The improved access that the railroad granted to Valley farmers had also made it cheaper for farmers from other regions, where greater economies of scale could be realized, to export grain to California. The Southern Pacific's decision in 1878 to shorten the primary transcontinental rail route by shipping cars via ferry from Benicia to Port Costa also took an advantage away from the Valley's farmers and encouraged the planting of more specialized crops.

Wine grapes had been grown in the Valley since the days of the rancheros, but the product had been intended almost entirely for home consumption. John Kottinger produced wine for sale by the 1860s, but it was not until the 1880s that the Livermore Valley began to achieve a reputation beyond its own confines.[101] It was an industry largely built on outside capital; although the big producers usually kept residences in the Valley, they also had significant prior business interests outside of it. A prime example was John Crellin, the founder of Ruby Hill; before planting vineyards in California, he made his fortune in the oyster shell business and lived in Oakland before establishing his vineyard near Pleasanton in 1883. Ruby Hill was probably the best known of the wineries in Pleasanton's orbit—most of the major producers, such as Concannon and Cresta Blanca, were closer to Livermore—but there were also several smaller producers, including among them not only Kottinger but also merchant Henry Arendt, warehouser Joshua Chadbourne and hotelier Jason Rose.[102]

The first golden age of Livermore Valley wines lasted until a series of shocks hit the industry, beginning with the nationwide business depression of 1892. Three years later, the phylloxera infestation that had earlier decimated other California wine districts slipped past the Valley's inspection regime, costing growers time and money as they replaced their damaged vines with the resistant varieties that had become standard elsewhere.[103] By the time they had brought the phylloxera problem under control in the first decade of the twentieth century, the vintners were faced with the growing threat of the temperance movement.

Unlike winemaking, the hop industry in Pleasanton was associated almost exclusively with one name: Lilienthal. Already known as a distributor, by 1887, Lilienthal was already involved in hop cultivation on the Joseph Black estate near the Laguna.[104] In 1893, the Pleasanton Hop Company was incorporated, and for more than a decade after that,

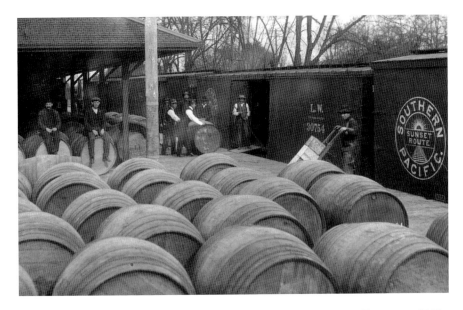

Barrels of Ruby Hill wine await pickup at the Southern Pacific station in Pleasanton, 1890s. *Museum on Main.*

Pleasanton regularly produced one to two hundred tons of hops each season. Pleasanton hops were purchased by so prestigious a customer as the Irish brewing giant Guinness.[105]

Unfortunately, the long-term prospects for hops were compromised by a reduction in the local water table, caused primarily by water exports from eastern Alameda County to Oakland and San Francisco. Both Lilienthal and the Pleasanton Hop Company separately sued San Francisco's Spring Valley Water Company in 1906 for damage caused to their crop yields by excessive pumping; in 1912, the water company brought an end to the matter by buying the affected tracts, providing a headstone for what was effectively a dead industry.[106]

Sugar beet agriculture was driven primarily by the establishment of a processing plant in Alvarado, in western Alameda County. After a few false starts, the Alameda Sugar Company had become well established by the late 1880s, and farmers in the Pleasanton area quickly seized on the opportunity.[107] By 1901, Pleasanton was shipping nearly three thousand tons of beets per year to the sugar plants, and the pulp left over from the harvest had become a significant problem due to the stench it created.[108]

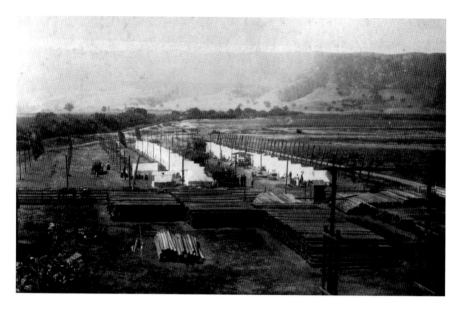

During the harvest, many hop pickers lived in tent cities on or near the farm, 1890s. *Museum on Main.*

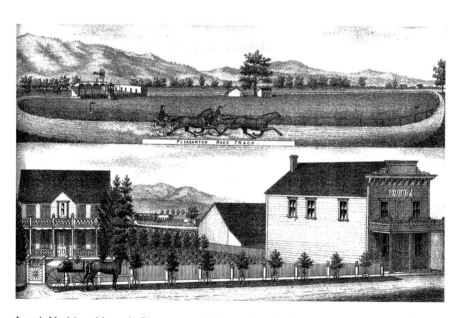

Joseph Nevis's residence in Pleasanton, 1878, as well as the Pleasanton racetrack, which he owned at the time. The home was on the west side of Main Street, south of Rose Avenue. *Thompson & West, Historical Atlas of Alameda County.*

All three of these crops required hand picking, which necessitated a large quantity of temporary labor at harvest time. Hop season in particular was noted for bringing in hundreds of transient workers, for whom special campgrounds were eventually set up. In the mid-1890s, immigrant workers—predominantly Chinese, Japanese and Portuguese—seem to have formed the majority of the labor pool, although local residents signed up for the harvest in order to supplement their incomes; hop-picking season was also touted as an economical recreational opportunity for city folk.

Although the Chinese Exclusion Act of 1882 formally barred immigration from China, there was already a large pool of Chinese and Chinese American workers in California, and the exclusion laws were not completely airtight (nor was observance of them universal). Japanese workers became more prominent as the decade wore on; by 1895, their alleged domination of harvest work led to a state investigation, revealing some unsavory practices by a Japanese contractor furnishing pickers for the Pleasanton fields and sparking a strike by those same pickers when they learned what the market rate for their labor should have been.[109]

Horse breeding and training may not have contributed as much to the area's gross domestic product as crops did, but its prestige value served to compensate. Two of Agustin Bernal's sons had laid out a racing track in about 1860 (as early as 1858, according to some authorities) on ground just west of where Pleasanton would soon be established. In 1876, the Bernal brothers sold the property to Portuguese immigrant Joseph Nevis, who had married their stepmother, Maria Juana Higuera Bernal (Agustin's second wife), after the patriarch's death in 1872. Under Nevis, the Pleasanton track began to garner more local attention; he seems to have held race meets more frequently and promoted them more aggressively than the Bernal brothers had. These race meets encompassed both saddle and harness racing; by the end of the century, harness racing would come to predominate. The track's site seems to have been wisely chosen, for experts regarded the ground as particularly suitable for horses; it also enjoyed the Valley's advantages in weather and easy access to high-quality local hay.

Industry

Although Murray Township's economy was overwhelmingly agricultural in the late nineteenth century, it did have one significant industrial product from the mid-1870s onward: bricks. In 1875, Joseph Black leased a site on the north bank of the Arroyo del Valle, about one mile east of town, to William Merrill (or Morell, in the spelling of contemporary newspapers).[110] Merrill founded a brickyard to process the good red clay of the riverbank into bricks to supply Bay Area construction. The Pleasanton Brick Company ran for nearly fifteen years before a slowdown convinced the owners to shut it down; however, it was purchased within a year by the Remillard brothers, who already owned a number of factories elsewhere in the Bay Area.[111] The Remillards had enough success with the Pleasanton plant to expand it in 1890, and it remained a significant employer well into the twentieth century. In the Merrill years, the brickyard hired a lot of Chinese labor, to the point that the *Livermore Herald* mused that the 1879 state constitution (with its various measures to discourage the immigration and employment of Chinese) would put the factory out of business.[112]

Law and Order

With the reelection of Harry Morse to the office of Alameda County sheriff in 1865, the cause of law and order in Murray Township received a considerable shot in the arm. Although Morse had spent his first two-year term just learning the basics of the office, he began his second one determined to bring down Alameda County's worst criminals. Even ten years after Murrieta's demise, Murray Township played frequent host to some of the most notorious outlaws in California; Narciso Bojorques, Tomas Procopio Bustamante, Juan Soto and Tiburcio Vasquez, not to mention many other, lesser-known malefactors, used the Valley and the hills around it as both refuge and hunting ground. By the time Harry Morse laid down his badge in 1878, none of the aforementioned bandits would trouble Northern California again, and Morse played a significant role in ending each career.

Beginning in 1866, Morse made a particular effort to acquaint himself with the full extent of his jurisdiction, spending hours and days in the saddle as he got to know its main features firsthand from

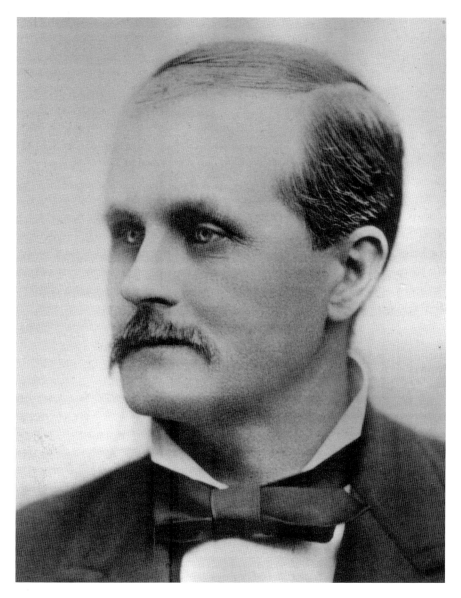

Harry Morse, sheriff of Alameda County from 1864 to 1878. The image is undated but was probably taken after 1878. *Museum on Main.*

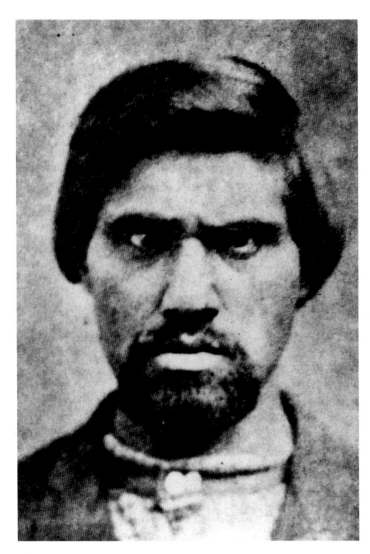

Juan Soto, killed in an 1872 shootout with Harry Morse; Morse was trying to apprehend Soto for the murder of George Foscalina during the 1871 robbery of Scott's Store in Sunol. *Courtesy California Historical Society.*

one end to the other, including the hills and valleys of backwater Murray Township.[113] Although the Valley's rising settled population encouraged greater social stability, the county's investment in its law enforcement infrastructure did not change much. When Morse retired, Murray Township still had only two justices of the peace and two constables, and only Livermore (incorporated 1876) had a town marshal.[114] One of those constables, however, was Ralph Faville, on whom Morse would come to rely heavily for support and whom he appointed deputy sheriff.[115]

Early in his third term, Morse nearly captured Narciso Bojorques at Scott's Store near Sunol, wounding him in the process. Although Bojorques would be killed in a gambling quarrel the next year before Morse could nab him, his sometime confederate Procopio did not escape: Morse arrested him in San Francisco in 1872 for stealing cattle from Pleasanton rancher John Arnett. The charge was not as serious as the several murders for which Procopio was the suspect, but it was a charge that Morse could make stick; after his release, Procopio would immigrate to Mexico and resume his criminal career. Vasquez, perhaps the archetype of the embittered Californio turning to banditry, was captured in Los Angeles County after an extensive manhunt in which Morse uncovered vital information but did not himself make the arrest. Juan Soto already had become a notorious bandit when he was involved in a robbery-murder at Scott's Store in January 1871; Morse would track him to the Saucelito Valley, south of Pacheco Pass, and kill him in the most dramatic gunfight of his career.[116]

Pleasanton and the Local Economy

As a railroad town, Pleasanton served as a point of contact between the Amador Valley and the outside world. It was an assembly point for agricultural products being shipped out of the Valley to the Bay Area and points beyond. It provided convenient hospitality for visitors to the area. And it served as a marketplace for goods and services that local farmers (and town residents) did not produce for themselves. While a few businesses had sprung up to serve these sort of needs in the years before the railroad's arrival, after 1869 opportunities expanded and entrepreneurs stepped in to take advantage of them.

One business that the railroad may be said to have created in Pleasanton was warehousing. Farmers needed facilities for the temporary storage of grain and hay shipments scheduled to leave by rail. The San Jose firm of Waterman & Company built a warehouse near the railroad depot in the 1870s, as did local farmer and lumber dealer Joshua Chadbourne.[117] Merchant Henry Arendt added a grain and a hay warehouse in the 1880s, and M.A. Whidden took over the Waterman warehouse.[118]

The hospitality industry in the vicinity may well have predated the founding of the town; the 1876 *Centennial Book of Alameda County* records that Charles Duerr and Louis Nusbaumer, upon renting the Kottinger property in 1858, "started the first public-house in the place" on the premises of a store that Kottinger had established.[119] (However, M.W. Wood's 1883 *History of Alameda County*, for which the author had occasion to interview Kottinger and apparently Duerr as well, notes that Duerr and Nusbaumer started the store after Kottinger left and makes no mention of any public house or similar establishment.[120])

A hotel was already in operation by the spring of 1869, before the rail workers had begun extending the line from Niles.[121] By 1879, traffic through the town was supporting at least four: the Farmer's, on the south bank of the Arroyo del Valle where it met Main Street; the Germania, on the northwest corner of St. Mary and Main; the Emerald House, on the corner of Main and Rose; and the Pleasanton, on the east side of Main south of Division.[122] In 1880, the Pleasanton underwent renovation and became the Rose, a name it would retain until its demolition in 1956. Herman Detjens, operator of the Germania on the other side of the street, immediately adopted the abandoned name for his establishment.[123] (After that Pleasanton Hotel was demolished in 1930, the operator of the Farmer's Hotel would step in to claim the name, ensuring that there would still be a Pleasanton Hotel in Pleasanton but creating an acute source of confusion for casual students of the town's history.)

Hotels provided for the rest needs of overnight guests; to quench their thirst and desire for conviviality, there were also saloons. By 1888, these numbered six, including the bar of the Rose Hotel. That number would climb gradually over the course of the next few decades, rising to thirteen by 1898 and seventeen by 1907.[124] And the saloons were only part of the liquor trade in town; in 1895, the first year after incorporation, the town collected fees for fifty-one retail liquor licenses—about one per twenty residents.[125] All of these establishments provided an outlet for the products of local vintners, brewers and distillers.

Other forms of entertainment did not go neglected, although most seem to have been less popular than the saloons. Theatrical troupes stopped to perform as they followed the rail lines from town to town. Local entrepreneurs organized prizefights and wrestling matches.[126] Some of the saloons, including the Rose Hotel's, featured billiard tables; cards and other gaming no doubt were available to saloon

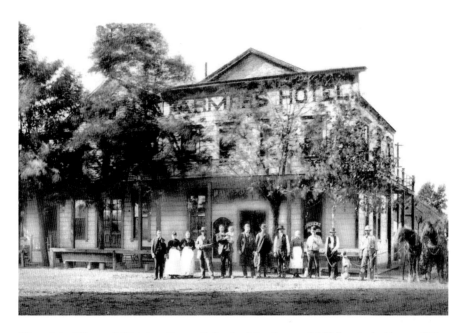

The original Farmer's Hotel on the south bank of the Arroyo del Valle, at what is now 855 Main Street. It burned down in 1898 and was soon replaced by a second Farmer's Hotel, which after 1930 took the name Pleasanton Hotel. *Museum on Main.*

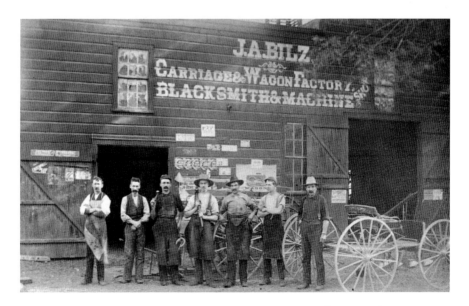

J.A. Bilz established his wagon works at 690 Main Street in 1868; this photo was probably taken in the 1880s or 1890s. *Museum on Main.*

patrons as well. The Farmer's Hotel put up a bowling alley between its main building and the Arroyo. In addition, prostitutes plied their trade in the hotels and the upstairs rooms of certain saloons. However, we know virtually nothing about the details of prostitution in early Pleasanton, for at the time the trade received little attention from either law enforcement or the local media, and it has traditionally left very little paper trail of its own.

Unlike the hotels (and, probably, the escorts), the merchants and artisans of Pleasanton primarily served the local population. The store, as noted earlier, seems to have come first—although that may be an illusion caused by the slim written record of the 1850s. We know that a smith and a carpenter purchased two of the first three lots sold by Kottinger in 1863; by 1865, a second smith, J.A. Bilz, had set up shop in town. Bilz was a wagon manufacturer as well as a blacksmith, and he would eventually receive patents for some of his improved wagon designs. After 1869, the expanded market brought new merchants and new artisans, most of whom set up shop on Main Street or on one of its side streets. In 1870, Bernard McLaughlin's store had competition from merchants Meyers & Landers and Walstein & Bergham, and several carpenters, blacksmiths and painters appear on the Pleasanton pages of the 1870 census, as well as a few saddlers, harness makers and shoemakers. Kottinger does not seem to have practiced law (except as a justice of the peace) during these years, but J.R. Palmer arrived in 1870 to provide both legal and notarial services. Further diversity evolved as the town continued to grow, including dressmakers and milliners, barbers and hairdressers, butchers and bakers. New general merchants came to succeed McLaughlin and the others: Joseph Arendt, whose family store would become a Pleasanton fixture from the late 1870s until the Great Depression; Hortenstine and Stover, whose location would later house one of the town's signature buildings under the name Kolln Hardware; and Philip Kolb, who began with a bakery in 1878 and by 1890 owned one of the town's foremost general stores.

Forming Community Institutions

Pleasanton remained unincorporated for the first three decades of its existence. In the absence of municipal government—and given the slim resources the county devoted to Murray Township's administration—the town relied heavily on volunteerism and volunteer organizations to develop and maintain a sense of community. Fraternal orders, churches, local newspapers and eventually a volunteer fire department helped to develop community identity in the years before incorporation, as did the local school—although the school was actually a government institution, formed under county auspices with local supervision.

Schools

Pleasanton's first schoolhouse was built within a year after Kottinger began selling the lots around which the town was developed. The Neals provided a site on the east side of Division Street, and residents put up $2,200 to build a one-room schoolhouse; within a decade, it would have to be expanded.[127] Joshua Neal was selected as one of the school's three original trustees, and a Mr. Powell was hired as schoolmaster. The institution was recognized as the Pleasanton School District in 1866,

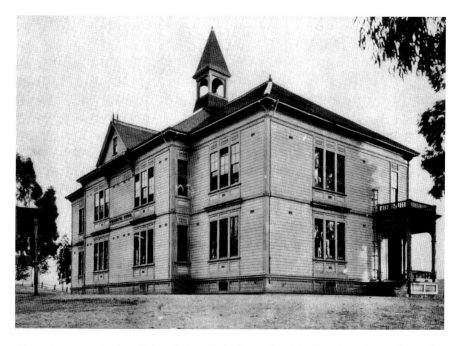

The eight-room school on "Knowledge Hill" at Second and Abbie, pictured here, burned down in 1909. Its replacement was built the following year and featured reinforced concrete walls. *Museum on Main.*

when the county split Murray Township's lone school district four ways to recognize the Valley's growing education needs and the establishment of new primary schools in Pleasanton and Sunol.

The school grew slowly at first; by the spring of 1880, its faculty had only risen to two teachers after fourteen years. From there onward, the pace quickened, however. By 1885, the size of the faculty had doubled to four.[128] Three years later, district voters approved a $12,000 bond measure to build a new facility on a rise east of First Street, near the south end of town. The new school on "Knowledge Hill" was a two-story affair with eight classrooms, a library, a speaking-tube intercom system and electric bells; there was also a separate stable for the horses of commuting students and teachers.[129]

The Pleasanton school, like all of the early Valley schools, provided instruction only for the first eight grades. Students who could afford and wanted a high school education had to leave the Valley, usually for San Jose, until 1891. In that year, the school districts of the Livermore area formed a union high school district; Pleasanton was invited to join but declined.[130] The Livermore Union High School opened its doors in 1893, with four students from Pleasanton attending classes alongside their Livermore-area neighbors. Some of these students, such as Lydia Minerva "Minnie" Rathbone, would later return as teachers to the primary school in their hometown.

Churches

A Methodist church was operating in town by 1871, but the congregation sold the building in 1876, just as the town's Presbyterians were applying to the San Jose presbytery for recognition of their own congregation.[131] The First Presbyterian Church was built at the corner of Second and Neal Streets, and it eventually became a local landmark. St. Augustine's Catholic parish was formed next; its church was built in 1882–83 on Rose Street.[132] There was not a sufficiently large Jewish community to support a synagogue, but there were a few Jewish families in town who observed their faith at home. The Chinese community does not seem to have established a temple (or "joss house," in the parlance of the time) until after the turn of the century, and the Native American community, though at least nominally Catholic, also observed traditional rituals at the Alisal Ranchería.

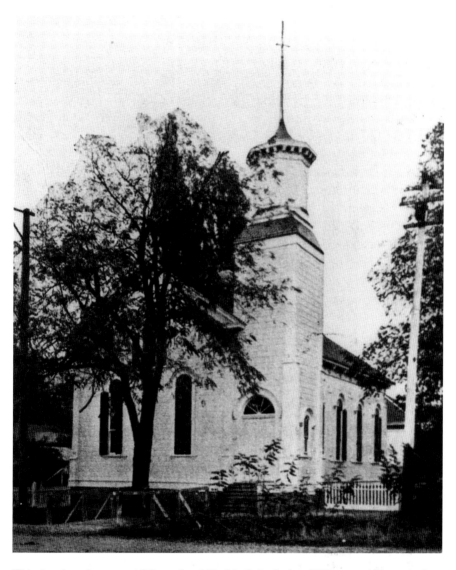

This church at the corner of Second and Neal, built in the late 1870s, served Pleasanton's Presbyterian community until 1977. In 1979, it was purchased by a Baptist congregation and has remained a Baptist church. *Museum on Main.*

Fraternal Organizations

Among the first community institutions established in the new town were chapters of fraternal organizations. The Freemasons chartered Pleasanton Lodge No. 218 in August 1871 with the encouragement of John Kottinger, who was a member of San Jose's Lodge No. 10. Its first members included such prominent citizens of the Valley as merchant Harris Arendt, wagon manufacturer J.A. Bilz, ranchers Joseph Black and Charles W. Dougherty and carpenter Louis W. Winn.[133] By 1874, however, it had become clear that Livermore would be a more convenient location for most of the lodge's members; the name was changed to Mosaic Lodge a few years after the move, and Pleasanton would not have its own Masonic lodge again for another two decades.

The Masons were followed by the International Order of Odd Fellows, which organized a local chapter in 1877. There does not seem to have been significant overlap between the two organizations; the Odd Fellows' charter members included Germania Hotel manager Herman Detjens, merchant and future board of trustees president John B. Hortenstine and attorney John R. Palmer.[134] Detjens and Palmer were also members of the Ancient Order of United Workmen, which had organized a local chapter ("Industry Lodge") by 1880.[135] These fraternal orders were primarily mutual-aid organizations, providing such services as disability and unemployment insurance for their

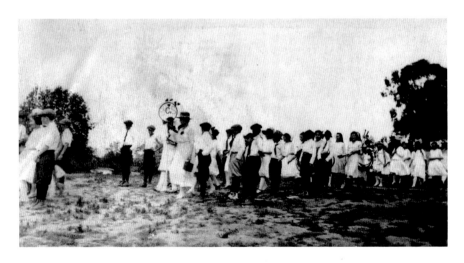

Boys and girls marching in Pleasanton's IDES Holy Ghost parade, circa 1910. *Museum on Main.*

membership. In pursuit of that mission, the Odd Fellows purchased land for a cemetery in 1882.

Over the next two decades, not only did the Freemasons return (Alisal Lodge No. 321, chartered in 1894), but also the Ancient Order of Druids (by 1890) and the Independent Order of Foresters (1899) established chapters in Pleasanton.[136] (The Foresters would in 1903 present the city with two oak seedlings imported from England's Sherwood Forest.[137]) In addition, ladies' auxiliaries such as the IOOF's Rebekahs appeared in Pleasanton during the 1880s and '90s.

The Portuguese community's fraternal organizations, the religious IDES and the Portuguese Union of California, established themselves in Pleasanton as the local community grew. The IDES formed a chapter in Pleasanton in 1898, and the Grand Council of the Portuguese Union held a convention in Pleasanton in the fall of 1896.[138] During the first decade of the following century, the annual IDES Holy Ghost pageant would become one of the town's biggest annual events, on or near at par with the Fourth of July parade.

Newspapers

Pleasanton's first newspaper, the *Star*, began publication in 1882; it ran for seven years before encountering difficulties from which it would be rescued by Sunol resident E.B. Thompson, who rechristened the paper the *Times* as of November 1889.[139] Over the next two decades, the paper changed management and ownership several times, merged with the short-lived *Bulletin* (1897–99) and became established as the community's primary source for local news despite the revolving door of its masthead.

Like many local newspapers of its era, the *Star/Times* generally maintained an editorial stance of easily outraged bourgeois respectability. Opinion pieces in the papers' few surviving issues warn of the dangers posed by tramps and vagrants, the excesses of the day's youth, the threat of unchecked immigration and similar small-town bêtes noires. The *Star* was also an early proponent of incorporation, proposing it as early as 1885, and also favored such measures as the subdivision of the Valley's large farms to encourage growth.[140]

Fire Department

Pleasanton residents organized the town's first volunteer fire brigade in 1888.[141] By 1889, there were both hook-and-ladder and hose

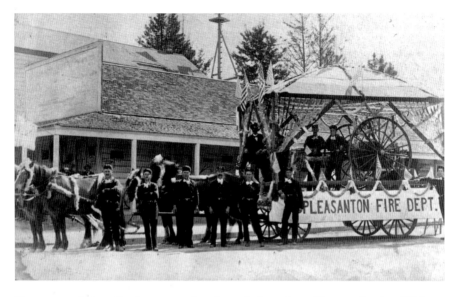

Pleasanton volunteer fire department float for an Independence Day parade, circa 1900. *Museum on Main.*

companies, the former housed in a building on Division Street near the railroad tracks (and next door to the town jail).[142] In addition to providing a vital public service, volunteer fire departments were an important focus of community social activity in the nineteenth and early twentieth centuries, especially through their fundraising efforts. However, it is not clear how prominent the Pleasanton brigade was in this respect before incorporation, for little documentation survives of its activities for the years before it was reorganized under municipal auspices in 1901.

Cultural Organizations

The first explicitly cultural organizations to appear in Pleasanton seem to have been literary societies. A "Pioneer Literary Society" and a "Whittier Library and Literary Association," which may very well have been the same organization, were meeting in Pleasanton in 1880.[143] Sporting and especially musical organizations seem to have lagged behind, perhaps because of their higher capital outlay, but by the middle of the decade, Valley newspapers were reporting the results of games—most likely baseball—between teams from Pleasanton and opponents from Livermore and Sunol. It is not always clear, however, whether these teams were connected to the local school or were organized independently by the community.

Politics

Early Pleasanton politics are so poorly documented as to be almost completely opaque. Any pro-Republican tilt occasioned by the Civil War had ended by the early 1870s, and both parties were active in the Valley. We know that there was considerable local sentiment against the revised state constitution in 1879, although it is not entirely clear which provisions provoked the opposition.[144] Before incorporation, political rivalries had to play out at the township or county level, and there are reports of both Democratic and Republican organizations sponsoring picnics and rallies.[145] Although the area was still so lightly populated that personalities rather than partisanship would most likely have predominated in local politics, the sketchy newspaper trail has left little trace of its outlines.

Getaways

Rail access also made the Valley attractive to Bay Area elites as a good site for a "little place in the country," an opportunity to live the life of a country squire or ranchero without having to depend on its proceeds for their living. These estates included some of the early vineyards and wineries of the Amador-Livermore Valley, as well as some ventures in raising racehorses. The latter business attracted mining magnate George Hearst; he bought five hundred acres of land in what had been Agustin Bernal's portion of Rancho Valle de San José in 1889 for the purpose of raising racehorses and other stock.[146] After his death in 1891, his widow, Phoebe Apperson Hearst, would remake it into her own country estate and primary residence. Other outside VIPs investing in the Valley included San Francisco political boss Christopher "Blind" Buckley, oyster shell magnate Joseph Crellin, Oakland liquor dealer Theo Gier and borax millionaire Julius P. Smith, all of whom established vineyards in the Amador-Livermore Valley, as well as Italian harness-racing breeder Count Giulio Valensin, who founded a stock farm near town in 1887 and died five years later.[147]

In addition to providing the Bay Area's wealthy with a location for country estates, rail access to the Valley also encouraged more temporary visitors. The hills separating it from the rest of the Bay provided a change in climate, warmer and somewhat drier in the summer, and the Valley provided picturesque scenery for hiking or picnicking, as well as occasional events such as the race meets. These attractions helped sustain the hotels of Pleasanton and Livermore alongside the business traffic that the railroad brought through the Valley.

Water: The Hidden Export

The rapid growth of cities on the Bay, most particularly San Francisco, created a demand for water that purely local sources could not hope to meet. The companies serving the water needs of San Francisco and Oakland ranged increasingly farther afield in search of aquifers and watersheds that could be diverted to city water systems. By the mid-1870s, the Amador-Livermore Valley had drawn their attention: the arroyos that fed into Alameda Creek and the Laguna between Pleasanton and Dublin suggested the possibility of greater riches, and indeed there turned out to be extensive reserves beneath the surface of the Valley's soil. Both the Spring Valley Water Company (serving San Francisco) and the Contra Costa Water Company (serving Oakland) began buying up land in western Murray Township from the 1880s onward.[148] The Contra Costa Water Company struck first, acquiring lands in Rancho Santa Rita around the northern end of the Laguna in 1880 and 1881 through its founder, Anthony Chabot. Local interests immediately recognized the threat, forming the Lake Pleasanton Water Company with the declared intent of seizing the property so as to keep the water rights in local hands (so that they could sell water to San Francisco and Oakland, keeping the profits, if not the water, in the Valley). However, the Lake Pleasanton group was thwarted when a judge found that it lacked standing to invoke eminent domain, and the drainage project on the northern Laguna went forth.

Spring Valley had already begun acquiring land and water rights at the eastern end of Niles Canyon (in Washington Township) in 1875 but did not extend its interests into the Amador Valley until the 1890s, after first acquiring rights and lands in the area around Sunol. From then on, it gradually bought up properties around the arroyos and the Laguna

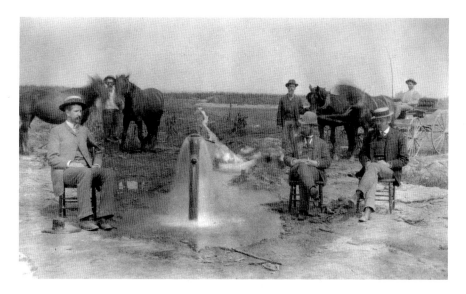

An artesian well in a field near Pleasanton, circa 1900. As exports to San Francisco and Oakland lowered the local water table, these wells became rarer and required increasingly deep excavation. *Museum on Main.*

until, by 1912, it owned a broad belt of land around the town's northern and western boundaries extending into the former Rancho Santa Rita (including land previously owned by the Contra Costa Water Company). It was drawing water from every arroyo and nearly every aquifer in the western Valley for San Francisco's needs. This massive export of a major Valley resource would soon create significant problems for Pleasanton and the farmland around it.

The Alisal Ranchería

In the mid-1860s Agustin Bernal gave his blessing to the settlement of several former Mission San Jose neophytes and their families on his portion of the Rancho El Valle, in an area southwest of Pleasanton.[149] Members of the community included Ohlone, Yokuts and Miwok speakers. Some members married into the Bernal family, and Agustin apparently provided material support for the settlement. It became known as the Alisal Ranchería, and although its residents worked occasionally for the rancheros as vaqueros and farm laborers, their

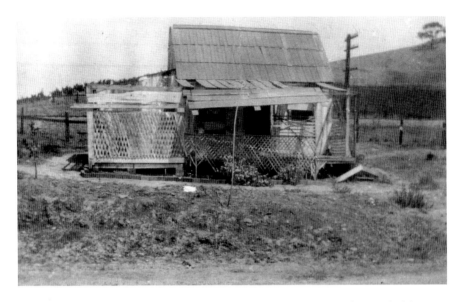

House at the Alisal Ranchería, circa 1900. This building was probably destroyed with several others at the ranchería in a 1914 fire. *Museum on Main.*

primary pursuit seems to have been preserving what they could of tribal lifeways. The ranchería comprised several residences and a sweat lodge, the latter playing an important role in the community's rituals and dances. These included not only traditional Northern California ceremonies such as the Kuksu world renewal rites but also, in time, elements from outside California such as the Ghost Dance cult.[150] In addition, they continued to practice traditional methods of hunting and fishing, plant gathering and crafts. They preserved old stories and their original languages. Along with a few other small settlements in the East Bay and a larger one in the vicinity of San Juan Bautista, the Alisal Ranchería contributed to a remarkable revitalization of central Californian Indian culture in the late nineteenth century.

After Agustin Bernal's death in 1872, successive owners of the property left the ranchería more or less to its own devices. However, the continuing development of the Valley economy gradually undermined what must have already been a fairly precarious existence. Without the Bernals' support, and as the increasing population led to more intensive land use, the ranchería's economic base slowly withered.

The Hearst Hacienda

When Senator George Hearst died in 1891, the fate of his horse ranch in the Pleasanton area was left in the hands of his widow, Phoebe Apperson Hearst. With a keen interest in education, as well as a considerable fortune thanks to Hearst's success in mining, Mrs. Hearst at first explored a plan of her husband's to build a trade school for underprivileged boys on the property. However, other philanthropic projects, primarily involving the University of California, occupied her time for the next few years. In the meantime, her son William Randolph, nearing forty and already a famous newspaper publisher, began turning the property into a pleasure retreat for himself and his friends. By the time she discovered his activities in 1896, he had already commissioned and begun building a villa; she quickly took control of the ranch once again and, after the house was finished in 1897, moved her household in.[151]

She named the estate *Hacienda del Pozo de Verona*, after a Renaissance wellhead imported to grace its courtyard. The house was originally designed by A.C. Schweinfurth in a Spanish-Mexican style; Hearst would later commission female architecture pioneer Julia Morgan to design additions and outbuildings. The Hacienda soon became the Valley's best-known architectural landmark. Hearst had a railroad depot (Verona Station) built where the Southern Pacific passed by the Hacienda; horse-drawn carriages brought her frequent guests uphill from the station to the manor house. These included not only personal friends and dignitaries from the worlds of academia and politics but also graduating classes from the University of California and, in 1912, the three hundred delegates of the Young Women's Christian Association summer camp.[152] That same year, Mrs. Hearst—a supporter of the Baha'i faith since the late 1890s—welcomed Baha'i leader `Abdu'l-Bahá during his tour of the United States.

The estate's lands included the Alisal Ranchería, the community of former Mission Indians that Agustin Bernal had welcomed in 1864. During the early 1900s, the ranchería attracted the interest of several anthropologists seeking to document California Indian culture in the fear that it would soon be erased. Mrs. Hearst was the primary funder of the University of California's anthropology department, and so it was natural that its leading scholar, Alfred Kroeber, would study the Alisal community. Unfortunately, Kroeber believed that the community's fusion of Ohlone, Yokuts and other tribal traditions

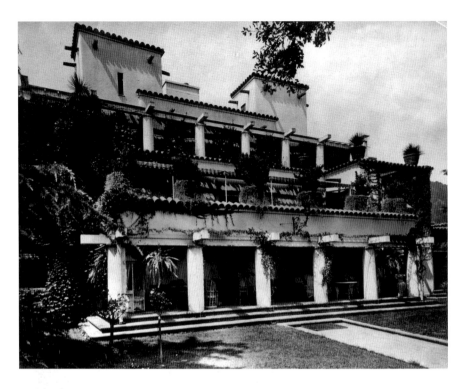

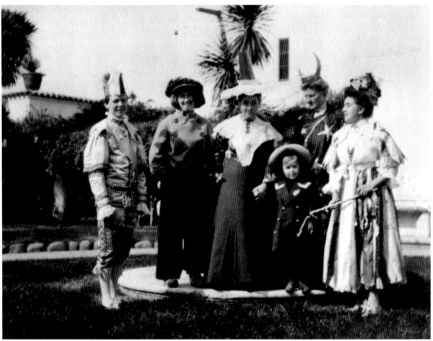

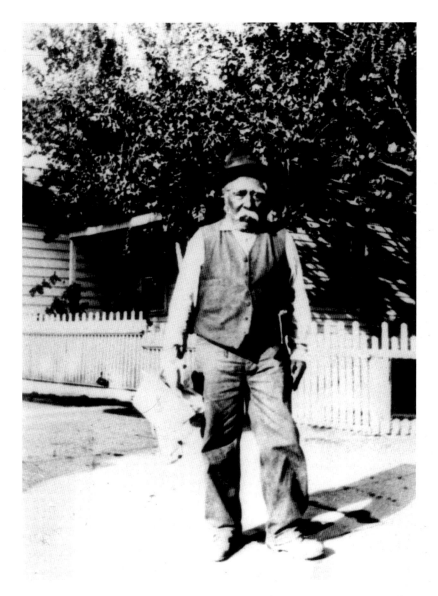

José Guzman was a resident of the Alisal Ranchería during its later years. In the 1920s, he worked with anthropologist John Peabody Harrington to record the native languages of the area, and he died in Pleasanton in 1934. *Museum on Main.*

Opposite, top: Façade of Phoebe Hearst's *Hacienda del Pozo de Verona*. *Museum on Main.*

Opposite, bottom: Costume party at the Hacienda. Phoebe Hearst stands in the center, dressed as Mother Goose. The boy in front of her is her grandson William Randolph Hearst Jr. *Museum on Main.*

made them unsuitable for study, and he moved on to other tribes that he felt had a less compromised connection to their pre-colonial roots. It would be left to a later scholar, John P. Harrington, to give the members of the Alisal community the attention their remarkable cultural achievement deserved—yet Harrington declined to publish his work during his lifetime.[153]

By the mid-1890s, the town of Pleasanton had enjoyed nearly twenty-five years of almost totally unregulated growth. Its population had nearly doubled, and it had developed an infrastructure of economic and social institutions that gave it an identity apart from the farming hinterland that it served as a market and depot. However, with that growth had come problems: social problems such as public drunkenness and rowdyism, health problems such as inadequate waste disposal and pest control and resource problems such as a gradually dropping water table. For many Pleasantonians, it was time to take control of these issues and, with them, the town's future by incorporating and thereby assuming the authority to force reforms.

Progressive Pleasanton: The Booster Years, 1894–1920

As the twentieth century approached, Pleasanton's leading residents took an increasingly active approach to promoting the town and its interests. Boosterism was a well-established phenomenon in American culture by the end of the nineteenth century: aggressive hometown promotion (and disparagement of critics as "kickers" or "knockers") had been lampooned in 1871 by Kentucky congressman J. Proctor Knott, whose speech "The Untold Delights of Duluth" became a national bestseller.[154] But the desire to grow and prosper, and to achieve reputation among a growing crowd of small towns and cities in California and the nation, spurred Pleasanton's leading citizens to embrace the booster ethos and scorn any "kickers" who might mock them. Establishing that reputation would begin with gaining greater control over local conditions by formal incorporation as a municipality.

Incorporation

The question of incorporating Pleasanton arose as early as 1885, when the *Star*'s publisher laid out an argument in favor of it that pointed out the advantages Livermore had gained by incorporating in 1876 and warned that Pleasanton might fall ever farther behind the rest of the Valley if it did not follow suit. In 1891, according to the *San Francisco Call*, residents of the area were still mulling the question over, but they finally presented their petition to the Alameda County Board of Supervisors in February 1894 with sixty-two signatures attached; forty-nine further signatures endorsed a counter-petition against the measure.[155]

According to California's municipal incorporation law of 1883, any community of five hundred residents or more, not already included in an incorporated municipality, could submit a petition for incorporation signed by fifty or more qualified voters.[156] The petition had to propose specific boundaries for the municipality and estimate the number of inhabitants therein (in addition to requirements for publicity and transparency). The board would have two months to deliberate on the request, confirm the petitioners' population count and adjust the proposed boundaries as deemed necessary; if all went well, the board would then permit a referendum to be organized. The measure had to include not only the act of incorporation but also a slate of proposed candidates for municipal offices. The electorate for the measure consisted of all eligible voters residing within the proposed municipal boundaries for at least sixty days prior to the election.

The issues involved in incorporating revolved first and foremost around taxes and regulation, although the authority to expand via future annexations was also a significant consideration. Incorporating would create a recognized town government empowered to regulate such matters as public sanitation, utilities, land use, business practices and so forth as a means of keeping Pleasanton a worthwhile place to live. It would also create an extra tax burden for its residents and businesses, some of whom might suffer a negative impact from the regulations that the town's government might enact. The vote was held on June 4, 1894, and the proponents carried the day.[157] Pleasanton was duly incorporated by the end of the year.

With a population of not quite 1,000 at the 1890 census (and 1,100 at the 1900 census), Pleasanton qualified as a Class 6 municipality under California law; this class included the smallest communities eligible for incorporation, ranging from 500 to 6,000 residents. A Class 6 town or city was required to maintain only a few municipal offices: a five-member board of elected trustees; a town clerk, who could double as the tax assessor; a treasurer; a marshal, who in addition to his police powers could also be entrusted with collecting taxes and license fees; and a judicial recorder to adjudicate cases involving municipal laws. Pleasanton's slate of pro tem municipal officers included trustees H.P. Chadbourne, Joseph Nevis, John B. Hortenstine, William H. Martin and William Napier; town clerk/assessor J.H. Neal; treasurer P.V. Wenig; and town marshal M.C. Donnally.[158] A recorder was not named, but the oversight did not seem to be regarded as a problem in this initial stage, perhaps because the town still had no municipal laws to enforce.

The board met officially for the first time in June 1894 and immediately set to work.[159] In its first several meetings, its members established business license fees, set tax rates, enacted basic sanitary and safety regulations, mandated street curbs, imposed a youth curfew and banned prostitution and gambling (except on horse races, of course).[160] They arranged for regular sprinkling of the town's dirt streets to keep the dust down, using a hired team driving a water wagon provided by the county. They appointed J.R. Palmer as town attorney and established a board of health, headed by local physician J. Hal Cope, to oversee sanitation and control the spread of infectious diseases.[161] Over the next few years, Main Street sanitation, collecting license fees and the water supply would become the board's primary concerns. Complaints about stray dogs led to the establishment of a public pound in 1901; in the same year, the fire department was reorganized under municipal authority.[162]

By 1901, Pleasanton had already had a fire department for more than a decade, with a firehouse off Division Street by the railroad tracks that housed the town's hook-and-ladder rig (and that may also have doubled as the town hall).[163] But many considered the department woefully underequipped, and the destruction of the Farmer's Hotel in a March 1898 fire gave further force to arguments for upgrading the town's firefighting capacity.[164] The new fire department consisted of two hose companies and a hook-and-ladder company, united under a single volunteer organization with a code of bylaws, elective officers for both administrative and command positions and an official relationship with the town government.

In addition to donations of time from volunteer firefighters, the town also relied on donations of funds to provide them with equipment. Municipal tax money had paid for the land on which the firehouse stood, but the firehouse, both hose carts, the hook-and-ladder truck and even the handsome fire bell purchased in 1903 were funded by residents' subscriptions. The department raised further money through events such as an annual ball to help cover the department's regular expenses and pay for protective equipment such as helmets.

The reform was sorely needed, and indeed it may not have gone far enough; the pumping engine demanded by the *Bulletin* in 1898 would have to wait until the purchase of a motorized La France chemical engine in 1917. But Pleasanton was a town highly vulnerable to fire; most of the buildings, including the big hay and grain warehouses by the railroad tracks, were of wood-frame construction. Even where kerosene or gas lighting had been replaced by electrical lamps, the risk of a spark or stray flame was high, and the art of fire-resistant construction was in its infancy. Major fires occurred with what to modern eyes would seem like alarming frequency for a town of little more than one thousand residents. This ever-present threat added urgency to the town's concerns over a stable water supply.

Securing a Water Supply

Before the mid-1890s, Pleasanton's water needs were handily served by sinking artesian wells at strategic points around town; the local water table was high enough that these did not need to be particularly deep. However, by August 1895, the old wells had begun to run dry, perhaps in part because of increased pumping by the Contra Costa and Spring Valley Water Companies (to supply Oakland and San Francisco, respectively). An initial plan to install a modern system with mains and pumps ran afoul of the electorate, which in 1898 voted against bond issues to pay for not only the water system but also street lighting and a public library.[165] Soon afterward, however, Dr. Hal Cope sank a well on the very plot the town had rejected buying and found a plentiful supply of water below the surface. A revised bond passed in 1899, and the new water system based on the Cope well was built the following year.[166] (In 1901, the land surrounding the waterworks would become the town's first designated park, named after recently assassinated president William McKinley.[167])

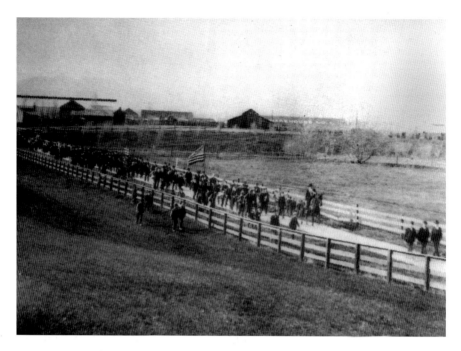

The dedication of McKinley Park on the grounds of the town waterworks, 1901. The park still stands at 519 Kottinger Drive. *Museum on Main.*

In the meantime, Spring Valley Water Company continued to buy up lands and water rights for San Francisco outside the Pleasanton city limits despite warnings from the *Livermore Herald* of the risks to the community.[168] The drain from the local water table cut into agricultural production, such as the aforementioned effects on hop cultivation. When the City of San Francisco, exasperated by its dependence on Spring Valley, proposed to dam the Hetch Hetchy Valley as the reservoir for a new city water system, most of the Amador-Livermore Valley applauded the idea.

Meanwhile, Pleasanton's water usage continued to outpace its system's capacity to deliver. Over the next fifteen years, the city would dig deeper and deeper, buy new plots for wells to feed the system and finally give up altogether in 1916, contracting with Spring Valley to provide for the city's needs in exchange for allowing the company to divert the Arroyo del Valle for deliveries out of the Valley. Prominent merchant Philip Kolb condemned the plan, arguing that the town should be suing Spring Valley for $1 million in damages rather than letting it suck even more water out of Murray Township, but the contract stuck.[169] Even then, however, concerns about water supplies remained, and in 1919, the town would invest in a magnetic needle for the purposes of attempting to detect underground water sources—a scientifically dubious practice known as dowsing.[170]

Closely associated with the water issue was the problem of sewage. Overflowing cesspits were apparently a common scene in Pleasanton in the early 1890s, and the town board of health's first report in January 1895 immediately called attention to the unsanitary conditions on Main Street resulting from inadequate measures for dealing with sewage.[171] Several years of digging extra cesspools and threatening laundry houses with eviction did not make any meaningful progress toward a solution, and neither did hiring a street cleaner. In 1909, one hundred citizens signed a petition requesting that the board of trustees adopt some sort of comprehensive sewage treatment system.[172] Over the next year and a half, the board developed a plan, negotiated a right-of-way agreement with Spring Valley Water Company so that sewer pipes could cross its land, found and purchased a plot south of town as a location for the system's outfall, contracted for the building of the system and enacted regulations for the sanitary plumbing now required of homes and businesses within city limits. Unfortunately, as with the water system, the sewage system ran into difficulties over the longer term; in 1918, the water processed by the wastewater treatment plant was deemed too high in bacteria content to be safely used for irrigation.[173]

Public Service and Its Discontents

Apart from the occasional (unproven) complaint about careless ballot-counting, there seem to have been few instances of public malfeasance during the early years of municipal government. The first town official to run into trouble was Marshal M.C. Donnally. In California law, a town marshal was required to post a bond guaranteeing his behavior in office; in Donnally's case, the bond appears to have been posted by Philip Kolb. For reasons yet unknown, in March 1896, Kolb withdrew his support from Donnally, who was unable to find another sponsor. M.C. Lyster was appointed to the job pending the upcoming election, with Kolb securing Lyster's bond as well. Donnally seems to have taken the matter personally; he withheld $245.00 in collected fees and then filed a claim for $83.33 in expenses and sued the town when it was rejected. (Donnally lost the case.)[174]

But Donnally's dispute with the town fathers was minor compared to the trouble town clerk J.H. Neal found himself in. Neal was Pleasanton's first town clerk and held the office from 1894 until October 1912, when evidence surfaced that he had misappropriated $1,577.30 from the town funds over the previous two years.[175] Neal (apparently no relation to town cofounder Joshua Ayres Neal) resigned his post immediately and submitted peacefully to arrest. He was apparently not regarded as a flight risk; the authorities allowed him leave from jail in November to attend his daughter's wedding. Neal pled guilty, and in March 1913, he was sentenced to three years' imprisonment.[176] Philip Kolb had been one of the guarantors of Neal's bond, but he apparently balked at honoring it; Neal's other guarantor, George Johnson, had died, and there seem to have been difficulties in recovering the funds from his estate. The fact that the board refused to renew the license on Kolb's saloon that fall may or may not have been related to the Neal matter, for in addition to the quarrel over the bond, Kolb had received warnings not only about the conduct of the saloon but also about his tardiness in hooking up to the town's new sewer system. The town finally obtained satisfaction on the Neal bonds from both Kolb and the Johnson estate in 1915.

The Valley Divided: Establishment of Pleasanton Township

By the beginning of the twentieth century, the population of Murray Township had grown to 7,172 people, with 1,100 living in Pleasanton proper and more than 1,400 in Livermore. Many, including the editors of the *Pleasanton Times*, argued that a single township was no longer sufficient for the management of county business in the Valley.[177] In 1902, the county board of supervisors agreed, creating Pleasanton Township out of the western portion of Murray Township, including Dublin and Sunol.[178] The decision created positions for two new constables and two new judges, nearly doubling the law enforcement presence in the Amador-Livermore Valley. It may have sharpened the friendly rivalry between Pleasanton and Livermore, for each city now held precedence in its own township—although Livermore remained the larger and more developed of the two. Perhaps more significantly, however, it created a jurisdiction in which Pleasanton was clearly the natural hub, a circumstance that would eventually help to complicate future relations with smaller communities in the new township.

The Women's Improvement Club

By the first decade of the twentieth century, social activism had long been accepted as a suitable outlet for the energies of respectable women, even at a time when the vast majority of American women were not allowed to vote. Women were prominent in the temperance movement, labor reform and consumer protection, good-government activism, promotion of education and many other movements to improve American society and culture. Indeed, Pleasanton had an excellent role model in Phoebe Hearst, whose efforts and philanthropy on behalf of educational causes were world-renowned.

Therefore, when a group of prominent Pleasanton women established the Women's Improvement Club in the spring of 1908, they were, if anything, a little bit behind the curve.[179] The club's early activities included pressing the board of trustees for improvements in sanitation, beautification campaigns that emphasized the preservation and planting of trees and fundraising efforts such as street fairs, as well as cultural projects such as maintaining a public reading room and publishing a special "Prosperity Edition" of the *Times* that aimed to preserve the history of early Pleasanton.

The club's signature achievement, however, was its campaign to furnish Pleasanton with a new town hall and library on the site of the reading room at the northwest corner of Division and Main Streets. The club offered the land to the town in December 1912, attaching the condition that the town should fund construction and provide space for the library within the new building.[180] The following March, the club requested that the board hold an election on a bond issue to pay for the new building. The election was held in February 1914, passing 218 to 40.[181] That summer, the board selected William Binder to design the new building and accepted C.A. Bruce's bid for construction.[182] Pleasanton's new town hall opened in January 1915, with the town offices in its northern wing and the club's library and reading room in its southern. It would serve the city for fifty years before it grew too cramped for its combined functions.

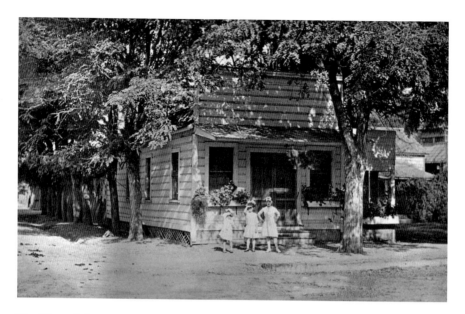

The Women's Improvement Club reading room at the corner of Main and Division, circa 1910. The building, originally a butcher shop, was demolished in 1914 to build a town hall and library. *Museum on Main.*

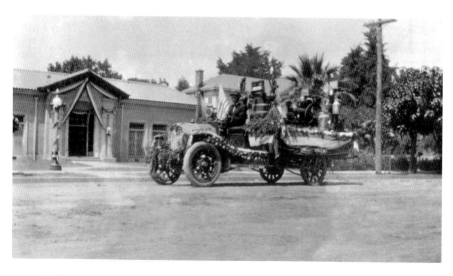

A parade float representing Cruikshank and Kolln Hardware passes in front of Pleasanton's town hall in 1917. *Museum on Main.*

But the Women's Improvement Club did not rest on these laurels. It campaigned to bring more trees to the town's streets, to have a local emergency hospital established and to improve Pleasanton's parks with playgrounds, gardens and water fountains. One issue on which the Women's Improvement Club apparently did not campaign, however, was women's suffrage, even though pressure to give women the vote was near its height—in 1911, it would pass by referendum as an amendment to the state constitution. In the Valley, the question of women's suffrage was widely regarded with suspicion, in large part because women were prominent in the temperance movement, and many people considered women's suffrage an opening wedge for prohibition. Local suffragists did form an organization known as the Good Government Club in the late 1890s; unfortunately, little information about its activities has been preserved.[183]

Finance Forward: Local Banking

Financial services in early Pleasanton were mostly provided by outside players, most notably Wells Fargo, which maintained an agent in town, and eventually in Livermore, where the Bank of Livermore was established in 1885. By 1893, there had developed sufficient population and capital in and around Pleasanton that a local bank seemed viable, and Edward L. Benedict began soliciting capital and organizing to found one that year.[184] At about the same time, a building and loan association was formed, with Benedict serving as its secretary. By the beginning of 1898, the bank had $50,000 in subscribed capital, half of which had already been paid in, and the building and loan association had issued its fifth series of shares.[185] Benedict served as the bank's cashier, and its board included such local worthies as onetime board of trustees president J.B. Hortenstine, town health officer Dr. Hal Cope and, as the bank's president, P.N. Lilienthal, who was well connected to Bay Area capital as well as to Pleasanton's hop and sugar beet industries. The bank building, erected on Neal Street near the Southern Pacific station, also came to house attorneys Donahue and Gale.

The Bank of Pleasanton was the town's only bank for about fifteen years; in 1910, a different group of investors founded the First National Bank of Pleasanton, which received its charter from the Treasury's Office of the Comptroller of the Currency in December

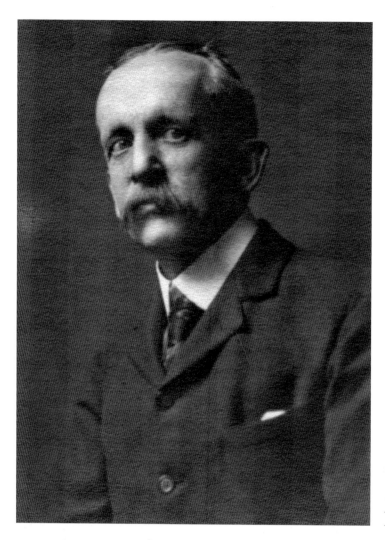

E.L. Benedict, founder of the Bank of Pleasanton. *Museum on Main.*

1910.[186] The new bank's local founders included Peter Oxsen, George Johnson and Edward Gunn; its first president was Pleasanton farmer and Clydesdale breeder Henry Mohr. The Bank of Pleasanton and the First National served as the community's only local banks until after World War I.

Chamber of Commerce

Only slightly before the Women's Improvement Club came the foundation of the Pleasanton Chamber of Commerce. Unlike the Women's Improvement Club, the chamber was established specifically to represent the interests of the town's business community; however, its goals of fostering a good business climate often coincided with the club's goals of a cleaner, healthier, more culturally developed Pleasanton. The chamber's first meeting space, as with many other new organizations, was in the old town hall, where the board of trustees granted it permission to meet in 1907.[187] In addition to pressing the board of trustees to adopt measures favoring the business community's interests, the chamber also organized events promoting local business and designed to bring visitors to town. The first of these, in 1908, was a Fourth of July parade (scheduled so as not to conflict with Livermore's larger one, however).[188]

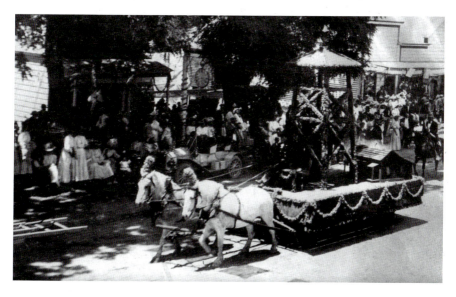

Pleasanton's 1908 Fourth of July parade, organized by the Pleasanton Chamber of Commerce as one of its first public projects. *Museum on Main.*

Expanding Transportation

By the turn of the twentieth century, the Southern Pacific Railroad had become an icon of the excesses of monopoly power and one of the most hated corporate entities in California. The promise of a rival transcontinental route prompted the formation of a new Western Pacific railroad company in 1903.[189] Partly by acquisition of existing routes and partly by new construction, the Western Pacific's owners (led by financier George Jay Gould) established a competing cross-country route by 1909. Part of the Western Pacific's planned route ran through eastern Alameda County, and the company negotiated with local landowners and municipalities for property and right-of-way. Both Pleasanton and Livermore worked out deals with the new railroad in 1906.[190] Soon afterward, in 1909, the Southern Pacific extended one of its spur lines from San Ramon southward to Pleasanton, with the junction built east of town at a place called Radum.[191]

While the railroads competed for the travel and hauling business of the Valley's residents in the first decade of the new century, the automobile arrived in the Valley. Cars began appearing on the streets of Pleasanton and Livermore in about 1900 and grew only more common as the years passed. They brought with them a demand for better roads, especially those linking the Amador-Livermore Valley with the rest of Alameda County. The proposed "Alameda County Loop" would run from Hayward through Decoto (now part of Fremont) into Niles, then through Niles Canyon into the Amador-Livermore Valley and then back through the Dublin Pass into Hayward. A committee of representatives from the various cities' business organizations (including the Pleasanton Chamber of Commerce) developed a prospectus for the project.[192]

After a few years of pressure from these organizations—and the successful arm-twisting of the Western Pacific to provide partial funding—a series of improvements to the Valley's main roads commenced, including the construction of a new bridge across Alameda Creek to accommodate auto traffic. The Niles–Pleasanton road and the route from the Altamont Pass to the Dublin Pass, running through Livermore and Dublin and connecting the Central Valley to the Bay Area proper, received the greatest attention. The latter road became part of the privately promoted, cross-country Lincoln Highway system in 1915 and part of the state highway network the same year.[193] (In 1928, the Lincoln Highway Association would shift the highway's route northward

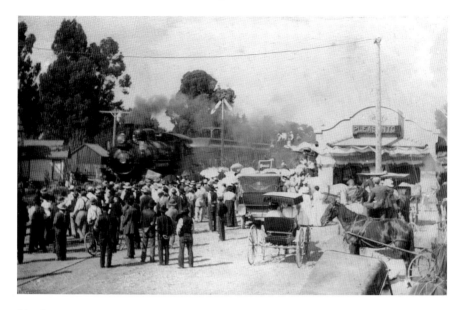

The first Western Pacific passenger train arrives at Pleasanton in 1910. *Museum on Main.*

through Vallejo and western Contra Costa County, but locals continued to call the Dublin road "Lincoln Highway" for years afterward.[194]) The year 1915 also saw the introduction of bus lines, both to compete with the railroads and to replace the stagecoaches that until then still covered routes that the railroads found too unprofitable to serve.[195]

As automobile transport became more common, and as cars and trucks grew larger and faster with improved engineering, road accidents became increasingly common and even threatened to crowd train accidents out of the local newspapers. The board of trustees passed a speed limit ordinance in 1907 and another in 1912, but they only applied within city limits, and many of the worst accidents occurred in unincorporated areas.[196] One of the most shocking of these incidents occurred in November 1917, when Esther Oxsen, driving her friends Wilhelmina Sylvia and Naomi Walton during an outing at the Fallon Ranch north of town, stalled partway up a hill; the brakes failed, and the car careered down into a ravine, killing all three occupants.[197] Although the crash was probably not the worst the Pleasanton area had seen up to that point (there had been others involving trains), the victims were not only local residents but also popular young women from prominent families, and their loss dealt a great shock to the community.

Bicycles arrived in the Valley only just before automobiles. Although its long-term effect on the geography of the Valley was less significant than that of the car, the bicycle's relative cheapness and mechanical simplicity made it popular for both practical and hobby riding. Bicycle races began to feature prominently in public festivals such as Independence Day celebrations and even the county fair.[198] By 1904, two bicycle shops were operating in Pleasanton: J.P. Thiessen's Rambler Cyclery, which also dealt in motorcycling supplies, and George and R.G. Brammer's Up-to-Date Cyclery (although the latter does not seem to have lasted very long).[199] Athough the craze for track and touring races had died down by the time the country entered World War I, the bicycle remained a popular form of transportation afterward.

Pleasanton's "Chinatown"

By 1893, Chinese businesses, spread along both sides of Main Street as late as 1888, had become clustered along a length of Main north of Spring Street on the east side and south of St. John Street on the west. The Sanborn Fire Insurance mappers identified these primarily as stores and laundries, although the 1907 map labels one building on the west side "Chinese gambling" and another on the east a "joss house" or temple.[200] At its height around 1898, this little "Chinatown" encompassed seven businesses, two of them laundries and the rest stores of one type or another.[201] These businesses employed little more than a dozen Chinese residents in 1900; several more Chinese immigrants worked as household servants or at the brickyard outside town.[202]

In later years, rumors would arise of tunnels underneath certain buildings on Main Street, and the most popular stories claimed that these tunnels had been dug by Chinese residents as a way to avoid curfews or provide secret facilities for opium use. However, although there was clearly prejudice against Pleasanton's Chinese population, there is no direct evidence to support the existence of a formal or informal curfew keeping them off the streets after sundown. Although signs consistent with excavation have been found in the basements or near the foundations of certain downtown buildings—not all of them historically associated with Chinese businesses—documentary or archaeological evidence confirming their existence has yet to surface.

The Dairies Step Forward

Dairy cattle had been part of the Valley's scenery since the first rancheros came to reside there. Even commercial dairying might be traceable as far back as the late 1850s, when a local market began to emerge as non-farming settlers started to filter into the area; certainly, several rancheros, including Francisco Alviso, kept herds of milk cows numbering two dozen or more. But dairy production was essentially for the local market; although Joseph Black might display prize-worthy rolls of butter at the state fair in 1873, it was grain that paid the bills on his vast acreage.[203]

Valley farmers only began to seriously consider large-scale dairy farming at the end of the nineteenth century. In May 1896, Livermore hosted a sort of symposium, featuring speakers from the state university and the Dairymen's Association, to assess and promote the Valley's potential for dairy production. In 1898, the *San Francisco Call* cited two "Alameda dairymen" who had been scouting the Pleasanton area as a potential location for a large facility.[204] The adoption of pasteurization and improving refrigeration technology greatly expanded the market

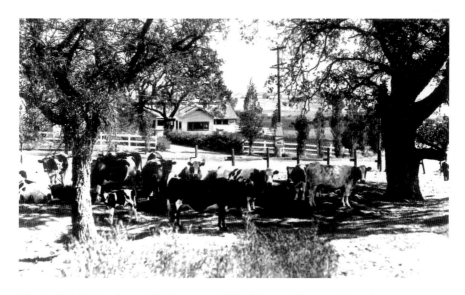

Meadowlark Dairy, along with Hansen and Orloff, formed the second—and more successful—wave of dairies established in Pleasanton. The Meadowlark's owners used this image for their 1930 Christmas card. *Museum on Main.*

reach of dairy operations in the late nineteenth and early twentieth centuries. By 1910, there was one dedicated dairy, the Rosedale, with nearly 350 cows producing milk and cream to be transported as far as Berkeley; various ranches also kept milking herds of 25 to as many as 200 cows.[205]

Media and Entertainment

In the late 1890s, the *Pleasanton Times* faced a rival newspaper for the first time in more than a decade. The *Bulletin* released its first issue in August 1897 and lasted for slightly more than a year. With support from two of the town's trustees, the *Bulletin* even won the municipal printing contract, although the publisher of the *Times* filed suit in protest.[206] The two papers consolidated in late 1898, rendering the decision moot, and Pleasanton once again became a one-paper town. Frequent changes on the masthead remained the rule for another decade and a half, however, until William T. Davis took over the paper in September 1915.[207] Davis

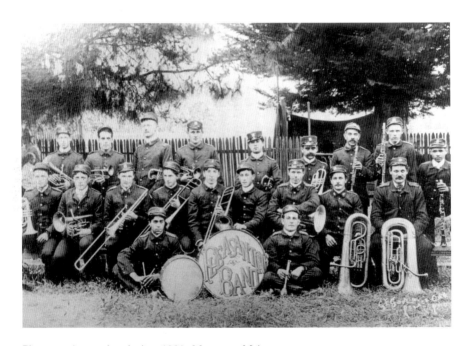

Pleasanton's town band, circa 1901. *Museum on Main.*

would publish the *Times* for fourteen more years, nine of those while serving as the judge of Pleasanton's municipal court.

The decade after incorporation also saw the establishment of privately funded civic cultural organizations such as the town's marching band, which was founded shortly before 1900, and sporting organizations such as baseball and football teams, which competed primarily against squads from eastern Alameda County but occasionally faced opponents from as far away as San Francisco.[208] A local boxing club was also formed in 1897, but many citizens considered the sport too violent for the town's desired image, and the board instituted a nigh-prohibitive license fee for public matches in order to deter them.[209]

Joseph Nevis provided the town with a dedicated entertainment facility in 1897, taking the reins of a project begun by the Bohemian Club, a social club that seems to have taken its name from Nevis's Bohemian Cafe (or vice versa).[210] The club sponsored a masked ball to open the Nevis Pavilion, and dances seem to have been the hall's primary source of rental income in its first few decades. However, the pavilion also hosted theatrical performances and benefit events, and it later widened its horizons to include such amusements as roller-skating and motion picture exhibitions. By 1912, however, Pleasanton was able to support a separate motion picture theater, called first the Gem and then the Lincoln.

A Golden Age of Harness Racing

The first decade of the twentieth century saw the Pleasanton racetrack at the height of its fame despite frequent changes of ownership. Monroe Salisbury, who had purchased it from Joseph Nevis in 1883, ran into severe financial difficulties in 1897; the track was acquired by C.B. Charlesworth, who formed part of a consortium headed by H.F. Anderson and including local breeder R.E. Lopez.[211] Their Pleasanton Training Track Company made further improvements to the facilities and then sold the property to Thomas Ronan in 1903. Ronan sold it in 1909 to H.E. Armstrong of Portland, and S.S. Bailey purchased it in turn before selling it to Winnipeg breeder R.J. McKenzie in 1912.[212]

Over the course of these real estate deals, the Pleasanton track once again became not only a top-of-the-line training and stabling facility for

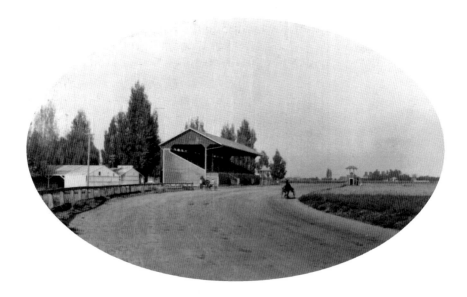

Harness racing at the Pleasanton track, circa 1900. In harness racing, the horses run at a pace or trot instead of at a full gallop. *Museum on Main.*

pacers but also a popular venue for race meets, including stages on the California harness racing circuit. The sport saw an upswell of popularity during the early years of the decade, and the Pleasanton track was well placed to benefit from the surge. Pleasanton hosted the opening meets of the 1904, 1909, 1911 and 1912 seasons, as well as several non-circuit meets in the intervening years.[213] By 1912, however, the public's interest in harness racing had ebbed again—a 1909 ban on bookmaking may have helped to dull their enthusiasm. Fortunately, racing men found another enterprise to which they could hitch their prize-winning trotters: the county fair.

Agricultural Showplace:
The District and County Fairs in Pleasanton

Before Pleasanton first hosted the Alameda County Fair in 1912, the town had a brief taste of the experience in 1902. Alameda and San Francisco Counties composed the First Agricultural District under the state board of agriculture, and for years, the annual fair had been held in

Oakland. However, it seemed that during the 1890s, the fair's organizers had increasingly neglected the broader dimensions of farming in favor of horse racing, and the district fair had become little more than another race meet—and apparently not a very successful one. District agricultural commissioner Emil Nusbaumer—son of Pleasanton pioneer Louis Nusbaumer and now a lawyer residing in Oakland—lent his support to a proposal that Pleasanton host the 1902 fair.[214]

The fair was held in late August, organized in less than two months by the recently founded Pleasanton Athletic Club, whose officers included town trustee Frank Lewis; *Times* editor Fred Adams; and local merchants Frank Diavila, T.H. Silver, Lee Wells and George Detjens. Short notice may have limited participation beyond the Pleasanton-Livermore area; when the *Pacific Rural Press* reviewed the results, its reporter characterized the event as not bad for a rushed first effort: crowds were smallish, betting was slim (though the racing was good), livestock exhibits were limited and few of the displays had come from outside the Pleasanton area.[215] Participation may still have been greater than the committee had expected; the announcement of results had to be delayed a day because there were more entries than the judges could handle in the time initially allotted.

The 1902 district fair seems to have been the last, despite Pleasanton's efforts to keep the tradition alive. Ten years later, however, another group of eastern Alameda County businessmen and farmers formed a new committee to organize a county fair. The committee included members from Livermore, Sunol, San Ramon and Irvington, as well as from Pleasanton; one member of the last group was druggist T.H. Silver, who had helped organize the 1902 fair.[216]

The timing may have been influenced by the recent announcement that San Francisco would host the Panama-Pacific International Exposition in 1915; certainly, the Alameda County Board of Supervisors soon appointed a committee to oversee development of exhibitions with an eye to the upcoming global showcase and showed extra interest in county fair planning as well. By June 1912, Pleasanton had been chosen as the location for the county fair, and plans were underway to build an exhibition hall on the racetrack grounds.[217] The dates were set for late October, more than a month after the state fair was scheduled to close, but the county fair was not intended to be a preliminary for the state fair, as it would later become. County officials agreed to display the exhibitions designed

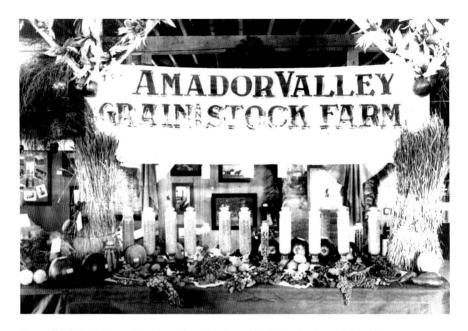

Henry Mohr's display of products from his Amador Valley Grain and Stock Farm at an early district or county fair. Mohr was also a breeder of champion Clydesdale horses. *Museum on Main.*

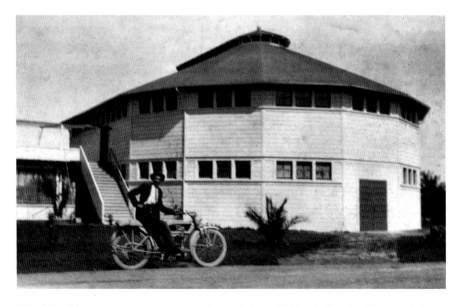

John Schneider poses on a motorcycle in front of the exhibition hall at the fairgrounds, in 1914. *Museum on Main.*

for the state fair and San Diego expositions at Pleasanton, providing an extra draw for audiences outside the eastern part of the county. These included a scale model of Oakland's new city hall, rendered entirely in fruit. In addition to the expected livestock, produce and other agricultural exhibits, the fair featured a Wild West show, various athletic events (including a baseball game), marching bands and drill teams, motorcycle racing and, of course, harness races.

The 1912 fair was widely deemed a success; the *San Francisco Call* gave it extensive and favorable coverage, noting the large number of visitors and the quality of the exhibits.[218] The halo carried over into the 1913 fair as well, but the 1914 fair failed to meet expectations and indeed lost no small amount of money.[219] With the big exposition in San Francisco coming up, the fair association decided (probably wisely) not to hold a county fair in 1915. It did hold one in 1916, but World War I prompted the cancellation of the 1917 and 1918 fairs, and the hiatus proved to be too long. By 1919, the fair association was moribund, and the track was only in use for private training.

World War I

At first, the outbreak of war in Europe meant very little to most residents of the Valley, except that the demand for agricultural products rose abroad, local farmers could get better prices and the demand for horses in particular spiked as armies bought up available supplies around the globe. However, once the United States entered on the Allied side, the Valley experienced a brief but intense burst of militant patriotism. A war board was organized to coordinate local contributions to the war effort.[220] There was a Red Cross donation drive, which earned the town a silk service flag. The local Boy Scouts started a victory garden, for which the board of trustees agreed to provide free water, and donated a portrait of President Wilson for display in the board's meeting room. Pleasanton schoolboys formed a pig-raising club to help boost food production.[221] And a local corps of "Four-Minute Men" formed to disseminate official news and government announcements; this group included such respected citizens as Dr. Hal Cope and former fire chief William S. Graham. By May 1918, nearly fifty Pleasanton men were serving in the armed forces, and a number of young women had volunteered for Red Cross service overseas, including Elsie Benedict, who in 1920 would be decorated by

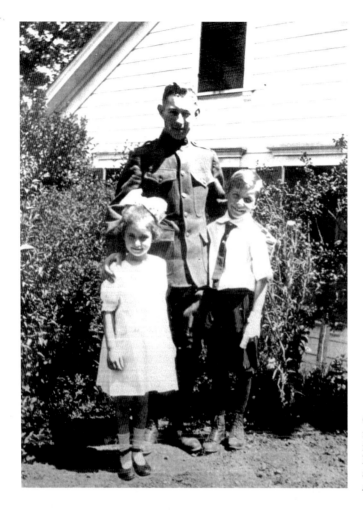

George Ziegenfuss relaxes with family while on leave from the army, circa 1918. *Museum on Main.*

the king of Montenegro for her work organizing schools and orphan homes in the war-torn Balkans.[222]

In addition to the challenges that mobilization brought to many American towns, the war brought Pleasanton some hardships peculiar to its own circumstances. The most significant of these was the suspension of the county fair, which had only begun to establish itself on the grounds near the track. That loss of business was compounded in the summer of 1917 when the board of trustees cancelled the town's Fourth of July celebration "owing to the unusual conditions prevailing throughout our country at the present time, and the uncertainty of the future."[223]

Pandemic: The Spanish Flu

The influenza pandemic of 1918–19 hit Pleasanton Township hard, as it did many communities in California. The town adopted the same countermeasures that many other communities had, such as quarantines, restriction of public gatherings and distribution of gauze masks. Early in the pandemic's second wave, in November 1918, the board of trustees decreed a fifteen-day emergency during which all public and private gatherings, including church services and lodge meetings as well as dances and parties, were cancelled; residents were forbidden to gather in public places such as stores and saloons except for the purpose of transacting business, and it was illegal to appear in public without wearing a gauze mask.[224] Quarantine measures continued until early 1919, when the

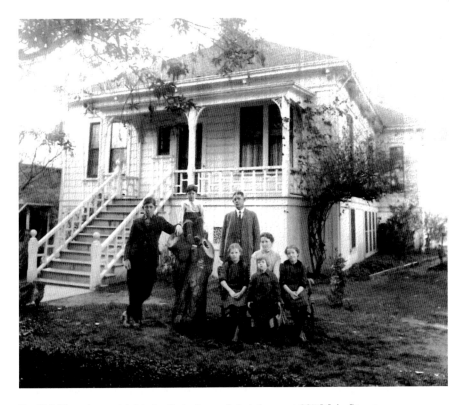

Dr. Hal Cope, here with his family in front of their home at 337 Main Street, was Pleasanton's health officer during the flu pandemic of 1918–19. *Museum on Main.*

board ruled that patients leaving quarantine would be required to wear gauze masks for ten days after their release. The masks were ineffective, although quarantine measures probably helped limit the damage. Among the victims, however, was Phoebe Hearst, who died in April 1919 as a result of complications from the disease.[225]

The influenza pandemic capped a sour ending to a period that had begun with great promise. Nearly all of the features on which Pleasantonians had based their hometown pride were gone or in decline by the end of 1919: the hop fields drained dry, the racetrack in disuse, the wineries threatened by Prohibition—even their famous and gracious neighbor Phoebe Hearst taken by the influenza. Although there was still a strong agricultural base and a citizenry committed to growth and improvement, the new decade of the 1920s seemed to offer the community more challenges than rewards.

Prohibition, Depression and War: Pleasanton, 1920–1945

Pleasanton entered the 1920s with significant elements of its identity in question. Prohibition closed down its saloons and threatened its wineries. Its famous racetrack had fallen into disuse after the ban on bookmaking, the collapse of the county fair and the demands of World War I. The great hop fields were dismantled by 1916. And even the railroad, the great enterprise that had brought Pleasanton into existence nearly six decades earlier, saw a rising threat in the spread of the automobile. In 1910, census takers recorded a population of 1,254 residents within the city limits; a decade later, that number had dropped over 20 percent, to 991.[226]

Who had left? The most significant drop occurred in conjunction with the decline of the racetrack's fortunes; horse trainers and grooms, numerous in 1910, are nearly invisible in the 1920 census. The Chinese community, already small and aging in 1910, drops from nearly thirty to barely ten people. A small group of Puerto Rican families present in 1910 also seems to have left sometime during the decade. Although the Portuguese community remained vibrant and numerous, its numbers had noticeably dropped as well. It is entirely possible that the wartime economy may have lured people away from Pleasanton for industrial work in more urbanized areas, although further research would be necessary to test the theory.

Economic Adaptation

After the passing of the hop boom and the enactment of Prohibition, the economy of the Valley had to adapt if it were going to prosper under the new conditions. Sugar beets and hay remained important crops, as they would until after World War II. The Remillard brick plant actually expanded its operations during the 1920s, remaining one of the Valley's noteworthy exports. But there remained slack to be taken up, and it would be pulled taut by commercial fruit and vegetable cultivation, the expansion of the Valley's dairy industry to serve broader markets in the Bay Area and California and the beginning of industrial sand and gravel mining along the road between Pleasanton and Livermore.

Fruit and vegetable cultivation on a commercial scale became practicable after about 1910, when pump-well irrigation was introduced into the Valley.[227] Tomatoes seem to have been the most important of these crops, although other fruits, as well as vegetable and nut cultivation, also played roles in this sector. By the end of the 1930s, flower cultivation, of roses in particular, had become significant, as the Jackson and Perkins Company began production in the Valley.[228] In addition to the seasonal labor required at harvest time, vegetable cultivation required more intensive weeding and other field maintenance than grain crops or even hops. The need for year-round agricultural labor brought Japanese and Filipino farm workers into the area as residents.

The dairy industry, which had gained a firm footing in the Pleasanton area after 1900, rose into greater prominence after the war and the enactment of Prohibition. Improvements in refrigeration had increased dairies' delivery range, and the decline of the higher-profile wine and horse businesses helped make dairying more noticeable on the township's landscape. Two major dairies were established in the years immediately after the war: Robert Briggs's Meadowlark Dairy, on the site of Francisco Alviso's old adobe west of Pleasanton, and the Hansen and Orloff Dairy, established north of town on the former hopyard

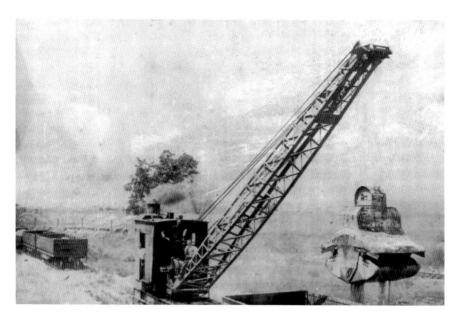

Scooping gravel into a hopper car at the Grant Gravel Company, 1919. *Museum on Main.*

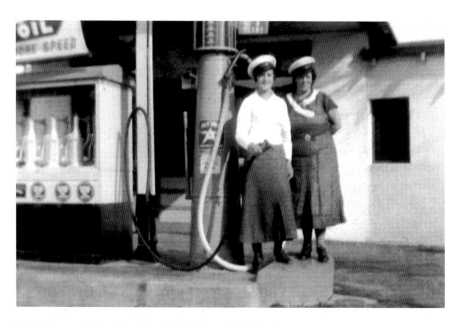

The Guanzarolis' Associated Service Station at 122 Main Street was one of several family-owned gas stations that opened in Pleasanton during the 1920s and 1930s. *Museum on Main.*

fields.²²⁹ Where Hansen and Orloff employed the pasteurization techniques that had become standard throughout most of the industry, Meadowlark was a "certified dairy" that sold raw milk produced under strict standards of safety and hygiene.

Gravel and aggregate mining came to the Pleasanton era with the railroads, which mined gravel locally for their tracks, but only became a significant independent industry after World War I.²³⁰ In 1923, contractor Henry J. Kaiser was hired to pave the road between Pleasanton and Livermore, now named Stanley Boulevard. Looking for a convenient source of gravel for the job, Kaiser found an excellent deposit of sandy alluvial soil right along the road that he had been hired to pave, at a place called Radum between the two towns. Kaiser started a quarry on the site and incorporated Kaiser Sand & Gravel to process and distribute it after his own paving job was complete.²³¹

Within the city limits, the growing number of cars in the region led to the establishment of several filling stations and garages. By 1931, there were at least seven of these businesses within or close to the city limits, serving not only local residents but also the many drivers who passed through town while touring or traveling between the Bay and the Central Valley. In 1930, the venerable Pleasanton Hotel, which most of the town had come to regard as a fire hazard, gave way to one of these service stations.²³² Christened the Amaral Tire and Vulcan Shop upon its opening, it outlasted all of its competitors in the downtown area and as of 2014 was still in operation as a gas station. The 1920s also saw the establishment of the town's first chain stores, as McMarr's and Safeway grocery stores opened in Pleasanton; the IGA (which was not a chain but rather the brand for the Independent Grocers' Association) soon followed. And in 1929, the board of trustees replaced the wood-frame firehouse on Railroad Avenue, in service since the late nineteenth century, with a brick facility designed to house the department's motorized fire engines.

Hollywood Comes to Pleasanton

In the early teens, Pleasanton's city fathers made an attempt to attract the nascent film industry, hoping that some company or another would establish a production facility in town. No studios took up the offer, but in 1917, a production crew from Artcraft Pictures arrived to shoot

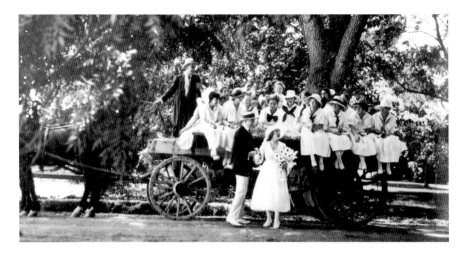

Filming the final scene of *Rebecca of Sunnybrook Farm* (1917). Mary Pickford and co-star Eugene O'Brien stand front and center. *Museum on Main.*

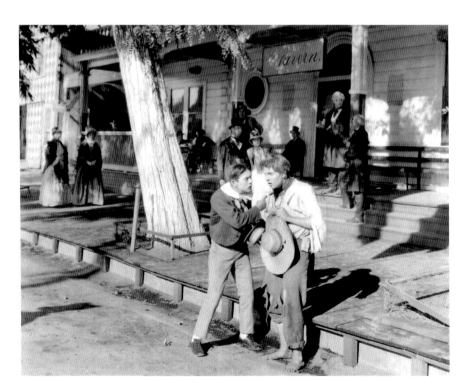

The Adventures of Tom Sawyer (1917). Jack Pickford (Tom) and Robert Gordon (Huck) in front of the Rose Hotel. *From the core collection, production files of the Margaret Herrick Library, Academy of Motion Picture Arts and Sciences.*

location scenes for Mary Pickford's adaptation of the Kate Douglas Wiggin novel *Rebecca of Sunnybrook Farm*.[233] Although Wiggin's story was set in Maine, Pleasanton's architecture and ambience were sufficiently removed from a distinctly Californian style that it could effectively serve as an Anytown, USA.

Finding such qualities in a rail-accessible town on the West Coast seems to have appealed to Hollywood's filmmakers, as over the next nine years, more than twenty productions featured Pleasanton as a shooting location. During this run, Pleasanton stood in for (among other places) Hannibal, Missouri (*The Adventures of Tom Sawyer*, 1917); Rome, Missouri (*Fair Week*, 1922); Eddysville, Massachusetts (*Lover's Lane*, 1924); Maple Valley, Iowa-in-all-but-name (*Woman of the World*, 1925); and Winnebago, Wisconsin (*Gigolo*, 1926). But the advent of talkies disrupted Pleasanton's film career, just as it did for so many other silent performers. The railroad that had proved so convenient for transporting cast, crew and equipment also made far too much noise for sound film. By the time recording technology advanced enough to liberate filmmakers from the soundstage again, the area around Hollywood had developed sufficiently that it no longer needed to send crews to the Bay Area for small-town charm; Pleasanton itself had grown up enough to wear the shine off of its down-home appeal. Between 1926 and the end of World War II, only two Hollywood productions are known to have used Pleasanton as a location, both of them adaptations of Damon Runyon racetrack tales: 1934's *The Lemon Drop Kid* and the 1942 Abbott and Costello vehicle *It Ain't Hay*. (Stories that the 1938 version of *The Adventures of Robin Hood* involved some shooting west or southwest of town have not yet been independently substantiated.)

Of course, Pleasanton continued to consume motion pictures as well as helping to produce them. The Lincoln Theater moved farther up Main Street in 1928 as the "New Lincoln" and began showing talkies the following year. By that time, radio stations were broadcasting in the Bay Area as well, and notices for radio programs began appearing in the *Times* around 1929.[234]

A High School for Pleasanton (and Dublin and Sunol)

By 1921, Pleasanton teenagers had been attending Livermore Union High School for nearly thirty years. Where four students were making

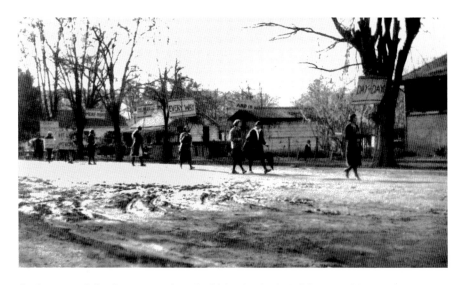

Students march for the construction of a high school, 1922. *Museum on Main.*

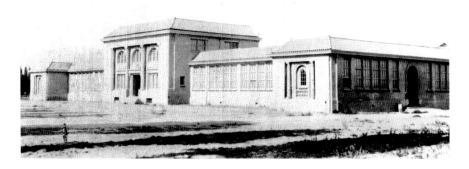

Amador Valley High School under construction, 1923. *Museum on Main.*

the commute to Livermore in 1893, there were now two dozen. Livermore High was nearing full capacity, and its administrators were increasingly disinclined to make room for students from outside their own district. In addition, students either had to take a Southern Pacific train running at inconvenient times (and costing $3.50 per month—about $45 in 2014 dollars—in fares) or take a carriage or automobile on a road that cars had made increasingly dangerous.

The Southern Pacific showed no desire to accommodate high school students, and an attempt to provide bus service faltered after a number of near-accidents with cars on the Livermore-Pleasanton road.[235] In March 1922, concerned parents and residents voted to establish the Amador Valley Joint Union High School District, covering Pleasanton, Dublin and the unincorporated area of Antone north of Pleasanton near Tassajara Valley. (Sunol voted against participating.) The district prepared a referendum on a bond issue for construction, and Pleasanton youth took to the streets to encourage its passage.

The location selected for the new high school was approximately a quarter mile north of the Arroyo del Valle, just outside Pleasanton's city limits on the road to Santa Rita. During planning and construction, the district built a temporary four-classroom facility on the grounds of the grammar school, the basement of which also served as the high school's chemistry lab. Fifty-nine students enrolled for the 1922-23 school year, two-thirds of them from within the boundaries of the Pleasanton School District and nearly all of the rest from the Dublin area; Sunol students began to enroll the following year. The contractor broke ground in August 1923, with the intention of having the building ready for use by the following March. The new Amador Valley High School was designed to accommodate two hundred students, but the plans also took future expansion into account, envisioning classroom space for two hundred more students, as well as a dedicated auditorium once funds were available to separate that function from the gymnasium.[236]

Hacienda to Castlewood

When William Randolph Hearst inherited the Hacienda upon his mother's death, he was no longer interested in maintaining the property as a country getaway; his own estate at San Simeon now fulfilled that role. A group of local investors purchased the Hacienda in 1924 and turned it into Castlewood Country Club, building a golf course on the ranch property and converting the main building into its clubhouse.[237] The Depression, however, gravely affected the club's finances; by 1936, it had been forced to reorganize, and in 1940, West Coast Insurance bought the property.[238] Soon afterward, West Coast sold it to dude ranch operator John Marshall, whose $240,000

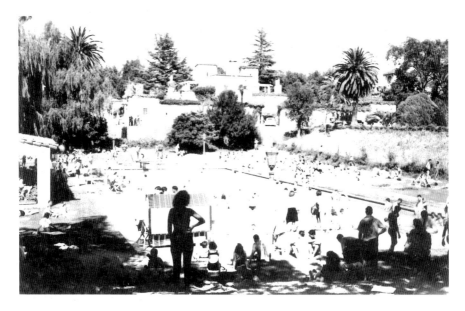

Swimming pool at Old Hearst Ranch resort, 1940s. *Museum on Main.*

bid had been refused in 1936, for $140,000.[239] Marshall and his wife rechristened the place Old Hearst Ranch and ran it as a dude ranch for the next twelve years.

Pleasanton Dry: Living Under Prohibition

Although the Volstead Act took effect in January 1920, California was among the slower states to pass legislation enforcing it—the Wright Act only passed in 1922, after an earlier law was overturned by statewide referendum.[240] The Pleasanton Board of Trustees duly passed a local ordinance the following year prohibiting the sale, manufacture, transportation and possession of intoxicating liquors; its terms conflicted with those specified in state law, however, and it was invalidated.[241]

Pleasanton had set its collective face firmly against dry legislation ever since the matter first came up for vote in 1874; that year, under the state's "local option" law, the town endorsed liquor sales in Alameda County by a three-to-one margin.[242] So although the temperance movement had gained a foothold in the community as early as 1871, its opinion remained deeply in the minority.[243] In 1915, the board voted not to support a bill in the state legislature regulating liquor sales. And though Pleasanton was far from alone in this stance, by 1919, the dry movement had scored its victory in the national arena—as well as in the state arena, as California ratified the Eighteenth Amendment in January 1919.

Between the wineries and the saloons, Prohibition had the potential to devastate the economy of the Valley and Pleasanton in particular. It should be no surprise that evasion of the law was widespread. Where possible, the larger wineries arranged contracts with the Catholic Church to provide sacramental wine and produced limited quantities for medicinal purposes, but these specialized markets were too small to consume anything like the volume of product sold in the pre-Volstead era. None of the local wineries seems to have adopted a dodge used by some Napa wineries: selling dried "grape bricks" that could be rendered into wine if one followed step by step the producer's detailed warnings about what might "accidentally" cause the juice to ferment. However, there was a lively market in fresh grapes for home winemaking, although neither premium grapes nor whites—the signature products of Livermore Valley growers—were particularly popular in this market.[244] In any case, the major Valley wineries cut back production severely. Only 1,500 acres of vineyard were saved during the Prohibition era, and the loss of experienced personnel would force the local industry to rebuild virtually from the ground up once Prohibition was repealed.

Saloonkeepers who did not simply close up shop converted their businesses into soft drink parlors—many of which could provide stronger drinks to trustworthy customers. As with much legally disapproved activity, it is difficult to say how many establishments continued to sell liquor under the counter. However, the extent of raiding from the late 1920s to the early 1930s suggests that many establishments honored the law primarily in the breach.[245]

Just before the Wright Act took effect at the beginning of 1923, Alameda County district attorney Ezra Decoto and Sheriff Frank Barnett warned their constituents that the new dry laws would be strictly enforced.[246] And raids in the unincorporated portions of the county seem to have been fairly common, judging from reports in the *Livermore Herald*. In 1925, Earl Warren took over the DA's office, and Prohibition enforcement took a new turn. Warren quickly built a reputation as an honest and zealous enforcer of the law, and reports of raids in Livermore and Pleasanton increased as county officials pushed harder against liquor trafficking. Warren also proposed preventative measures such as a county ordinance

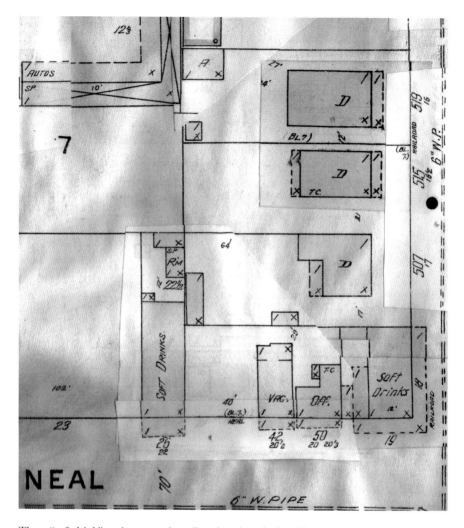

These "soft drink" parlors near the railroad station, depicted here on the 1929 Sanborn Fire Insurance Map, were saloons before the war and most likely still were saloons to those who knew how to ask. *Museum on Main.*

strictly regulating dance halls in unincorporated areas; these operations all too frequently provided liquor under the cover of soft drink sales, and so Warren proposed to ban the sale of all drinks at dance halls in addition to requiring permits and a strict 1:00 a.m. closing time for all public dances held in unincorporated Alameda County.[247]

The Parks Era at the Times

In the middle of 1929, after nearly fifteen years as its publisher, Judge William T. Davis sold the *Times* to *Niles Township Register* publisher Norman H. Parks, inaugurating a short but colorful era in the paper's history and inspiring the paper's first local rival since 1898.[248] Parks distinguished himself from his predecessor by raising the *Times'* page count (mostly to accommodate more news from Washington Township) and through his bombastic editorials, which he moved to the front page of the paper. Parks railed against everything from the slackness of Governor James Rolph's administration to the barbarity of prizefighting and the histrionic gyrations of the conductors of movie theater orchestras. Like his predecessors, he stood for middle-class property and respectability; among his favorite targets were the political and personal misdeeds of the rich and the privileged. Beginning his tenure as a committed "dry" and a Progressive Republican, he nonetheless endorsed Roosevelt in 1932 and accepted the repeal of Prohibition with some grace—although within a year he would be lambasting both anew.[249]

Having the town newspaper in the hands of an outsider and a "dry" apparently created market space for a second local newspaper. Or such was the thinking of Lloyd Rhodes and Jack Bullene, who started "a Pleasanton paper for Pleasanton people" in the summer of 1932.[250] The *Pleasanton News* declared itself in favor of bringing back horse racing, building a municipal pool, "modifying" Prohibition, improving local sewage treatment, reducing taxes at all levels of government and "state rights"—the meaning of the last phrase probably having more to do with income tax and Prohibition than with civil rights for minorities.[251] Rhodes was an experienced newspaperman who had come to Pleasanton from Ohio, and his editorial stance may have involved a certain degree of playing to his audience. The *News* was published weekly from July 15 to at least November 3, but a complete set does not seem to have survived. *Livermore Journal* publisher R.R. Kingsley purchased the paper from Rhodes in March 1933; by 1935, both the *News* and the *Journal* had been merged with the *Washington Township Recorder* to form the *Southern Alameda County News*.[252]

Pleasanton Faces the Great Depression

The first effect of the crash to be felt in Pleasanton Township was a drop in agricultural prices. Local dairies briefly investigated bankruptcy protection in early 1931 after cheese factories cut the prices they offered milk producers to 6.5 cents per gallon, 3.5 cents below the cost of production.[253] By 1932, the Meadowlark Dairy had filed for dissolution of its corporate organization, although the dairy itself seems to have remained in business.[254] Apricot growers put up their fruit for drying when canners' offers similarly proved too low, and the county's produce farmers formed a marketing association in an attempt to boost their negotiating position. A rise in foreclosures over the course of the early 1930s, as well as above-average levels of tax delinquency, testified to the difficulties facing local landowners. The Arendt general store, a Pleasanton landmark since the 1870s, closed up shop for good in the summer of 1932.[255] The town's major banks remained solvent, although the smaller Amador Valley Savings Bank collapsed.

The Valley, with its smaller population, had a much smaller number of unemployed residents than other parts of Alameda County. Many found work on the Hetch Hetchy dam and aqueduct projects, which had begun in 1914 and would not be completed until 1938.[256] County road maintenance and improvement projects also helped cushion the impact of unemployment, and county authorities consciously employed public works projects as a way to keep Alameda County residents working. A veterans' memorial building on Main Street, financed by subscription in a campaign organized by the local American Legion chapter, also briefly helped keep men employed.[257] Nonetheless, both farmers and townsfolk eagerly grasped at New Deal programs as the Roosevelt administration made them available; applications for federal farm loans streamed out from the Valley, while Pleasanton businesses jumped to comply with the standards outlined in the National Recovery Act.

The Valley's position as a corridor between the San Francisco Bay and the Central Valley brought a lot of unemployed workers through the area during these years, and as is common in such times, residents tended to regard them with as much suspicion as compassion. The county tightened its residency requirements for assistance programs in 1931;[258] the city council closed the Pleasanton municipal campgrounds and fenced it off in the spring of 1933, so as to discourage transients.[259]

"Feed them and pass them on," urged Norman Parks in a January 1932 editorial.[260]

Their concerns were sustained by stories of labor unrest and radical agitation elsewhere in California. Labor unrest such as the 1933 peapickers' strike in Washington Township, put down by police action, and the general strike of 1934 that grew out of the San Francisco longshoremen's strike heightened the fears of local authorities and landowners alike.[261] During the 1934 strike, the Alameda County sheriff and district attorney asked local police forces, even as far east as Pleasanton and Livermore, to provide extra security against the possibility of violence by radical strikers—violence that never materialized in the Valley.[262] However, some threats did hit closer to home, vaporous though they might be. In late September 1931, the manager of the Pleasanton McMarr's had an argument with a labor activist, who eventually left muttering dark threats. The next morning, the manager's wife found a note, rolled up in a large-caliber shell, on the front porch of their house. It read, "1 More Day" and was signed, "The Phantom," with a red skull and crossbones for emphasis. The stranger was traced to a local auto camp but never found, and the threat never materialized into actual violence.[263]

Community Service: The Lions and the Jaycees

The Depression era brought two new community service organizations to Pleasanton to stand alongside the old fraternal organizations and those founded in the Progressive era. Lions Club International chartered a Pleasanton chapter in the spring of 1930, with Jerome Arendt voted president.[264] The following year, younger local businessmen including Andrew Greve and John Amaral formed a Junior Chamber of Commerce. Both the Lions and the Jaycees threw themselves into projects almost immediately. The Lions began by sponsoring Pleasanton's float in Livermore's 1930 Fourth of July parade; they followed up with advocacy for road safety projects, the construction of a regional hospital in Pleasanton and reviving the locally moribund Boy Scouts. Not to be outdone, in 1932 the Pleasanton Jaycees took on the burden of organizing a three-day Fourth of July celebration, including not only a parade but also street dances, a horse show and races.[265]

That same summer, the Women's Improvement Club proposed a boosting idea of its own, in line with its tradition of making Pleasanton

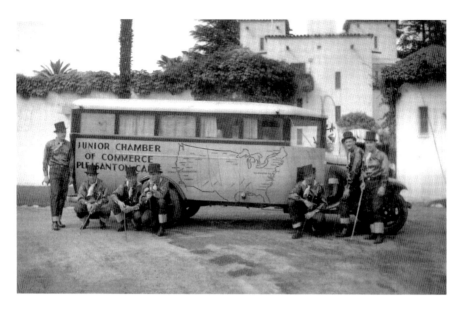

The Pleasanton Jaycees Travel Group prepares for a road trip, 1940. *Museum on Main.*

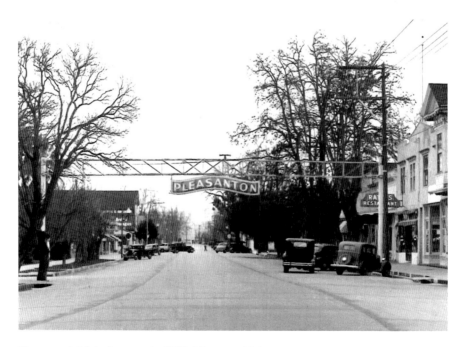

Pleasanton's Main Street arch, 1937. *Museum on Main.*

a nicer and more attractive place to live: a neon arch sign featuring the town's name to span Main Street. The club's members offered to purchase the sign if the city would pay for the poles to support it. Because there was only one sign instead of two, the city and the club agreed to place it about midway up Main Street—right in front of city hall at the corner of Main and Division. The sign was dedicated on March 8, 1932, and it eventually became one of Pleasanton's most distinctive landmarks.[266]

The Return of Wine and Wagers

The search for ways to generate business activity lent force to the arguments of those advocating the repeal of prohibitions on both alcohol and gambling, and Pleasanton was especially well placed to benefit from both movements. In 1933, a state referendum legalized parimutuel betting (in which odds are controlled by actual bets placed rather than by bookmakers), and over the next several years, racetracks sprang up all over California: Bay Meadows and Santa Anita in 1934, Del Mar in 1937 and Golden Gate Fields in 1941. The Pleasanton track was initially near the front of the line for this renaissance; it was purchased in 1933 by an East Coast syndicate with the intent of making it over into a major racing facility.[267] The syndicate immediately sent out a new manager to oversee the project, but the death of one of the principal partners suspended any major undertakings indefinitely.

Nonetheless, Pleasanton's profile as a stabling and training center received a further boost, and owners from outside the area sent more and more horses to winter at the Pleasanton facilities. While the Jaycees negotiated with the track ownership and the state racing board to bring betting races back to the Pleasanton track, Pleasanton sent its horses to Tanforan and Bay Meadows to compete. The return of racing to Pleasanton would have to wait until the revival of the county fair at the end of the decade.

The repeal of the Eighteenth Amendment, and with it the laws mandating Prohibition, came at the end of 1933. Because alcohol sales did not require the cooperation of a local monopoly, business was more nimble in reaching for the opportunities that this repeal offered. In an attempt to echo the Valley's past glories as a wine-producing region, the Pleasanton Jaycees organized a "Fiesta del Vino" in the fall of 1935.[268]

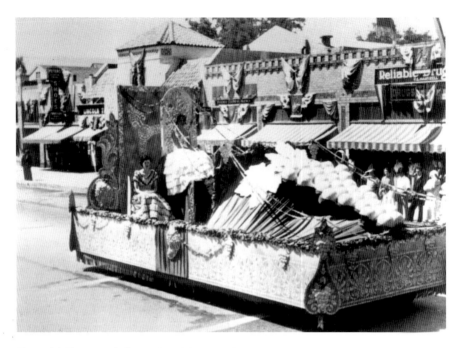

Fiesta del Vino parade float, 1935. *Museum on Main.*

This event adopted a Californio theme for its celebration of the Valley's wines and featured performers in "Spanish" costume in its events and parade. With Livermore's participation, the event was deemed successful enough to repeat the following year, in 1937 and in 1938 as well. In fact, Pleasanton might well have become known as the "home of Fiesta del Vino" had the revival of the Alameda County Fair in 1939 not created a visitor attraction with broader and more obvious appeal.

The County Fair Returns

The groundwork for the revival of the county fair was laid in 1936 when Crawford Letham, Jim Trimingham and Ernest Schween—all prominent local businessmen—decided to commit their own funds to bringing the fair back to Pleasanton.[269] The Alameda County Fair and Racing Association was established that spring. After about two years of promoting and agitating, the association convinced the board of supervisors to provide financial support from county funds and make

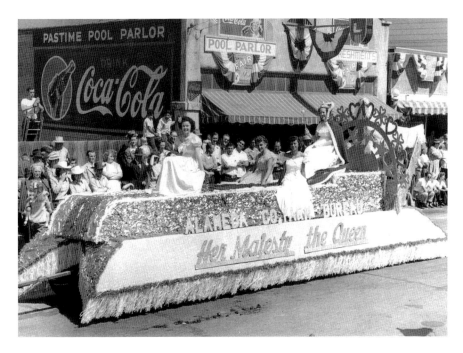

Alameda County Fair queen Mavis Williams and attendants in the 1938 fair parade. *Museum on Main.*

Pleasanton the site of the fair after defeating a campaign on behalf of Hayward. Negotiations with the track ownership proved difficult once again, but by 1939, all the elements were back in place for Pleasanton to show off Alameda County's best.

Unlike the fairs of the 1910s, the new Alameda County Fair was scheduled to take place before the state fair in Sacramento, so that its exhibition winners could represent the county at the state level. The organization of local 4-H clubs in the late 1920s opened a new avenue for youth participation and competition. The "Maid of Alameda County" contest, a beauty pageant whose winner would compete in Sacramento for the title "Maid of California," appeared on the program for the first time.[270] And the horse racing program expanded to include saddle races with Thoroughbreds and quarter-horses as well as harness races, all charged with extra excitement by the opportunity to bet on the results. The 1939 fair was well attended, netting seventy-eight dollars in profits in addition to any extra business the event brought into town, and prospects for the fair's future looked bright once more.[271]

Unfortunately, after two more successful years, yet another world war forced the county fair to go on hiatus, this time for three years. However, in this instance, the fair association was able to pick up where it left off, and from 1945 onward, the county fair remained an annual Pleasanton tradition.

Pleasanton Goes to War, 1942–1945

The advent of World War II brought major changes to the life of the Valley, much more so than the previous world war had. American involvement in World War I had been brief, and although its mobilization put local men in uniform, cancelled major events and occasioned a spate of patriotic lectures and propaganda updates, it did not much change the local landscape or the overall composition of the local population. World War II, on the other hand, resulted both in an expansion of construction and in the removal of one ethnic minority and its replacement by temporary workers from another. The establishment of military bases near town brought a large and rapidly rotating influx of servicemen and servicewomen, for whom Pleasanton could provide entertainment opportunities when circumstances precluded the longer trip to Oakland or San Francisco. In addition, a considerably larger number of local residents served overseas during this war than during the previous one.

MILITARY BASES

The attack on Pearl Harbor caught the United States unprepared for a major conflict; it had to mobilize both human and material resources very rapidly. The armed forces would need new facilities to process and train hundreds of thousands of incoming recruits and draftees, and authorities sought places where land was inexpensive and necessary resources such as a water supply were readily available. One of the locations fitting their criteria lay in the Amador Valley, east of Dublin and north of Highway 50. This site would become home to three naval bases: the Seabee training facility known as Camp Parks, a waystation ("personnel distribution center" in the navy's terminology) called Camp Shoemaker and a medical facility named Shoemaker Naval Hospital. In addition to a naval air training base east of Livermore, these sites would temporarily bring tens of thousands of sailors and navy officers into the Valley.[272]

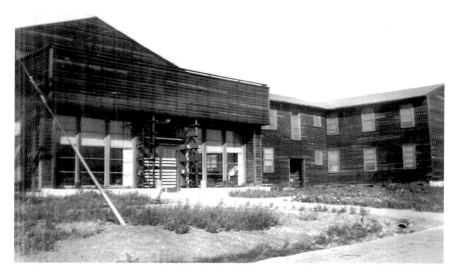

Barracks entrance at Camp Shoemaker, circa 1945. *Museum on Main.*

JAPANESE REMOVAL

In the 1890s, transient Japanese laborers made up a notable portion of the workforce in Pleasanton's hop and beet fields; like the Chinese before them, they were met with hostility and racism, and few made their residence in the area. After the introduction of pump-well irrigation systems around 1910, vegetable and flower gardening became more prominent in Pleasanton Township agriculture, and a small community of Japanese gardeners, managers and farm workers grew. In 1940, this community numbered about sixty people.[273]

Several weeks after the attack at Pearl Harbor, suspicion fell on the loyalties of Japanese Americans both naturalized and native. The reasons had more to do with racism and wartime hysteria than with any actual threat; there was little evidence that Japanese immigrants or their children might become engaged in espionage or subversion. But public pressure for action mounted, large sectors of the media warned against the Japanese threat and the U.S. Army's commander on the West Coast, General John DeWitt, announced that he considered all Japanese Americans, immigrant or native-born citizen, a danger to the country.[274]

Roosevelt had already invoked the Alien Enemies Act of 1798 immediately after Pearl Harbor to impose constraints on the movement and freedom of German, Italian and Japanese nationals. However, many German and Italian immigrants had become naturalized citizens and were therefore exempt; Japanese immigrants were not eligible for citizenship, and thus all of them were subject to having their whereabouts and activities tracked. These orders were soon expanded to include native-born citizens of Japanese descent.

A series of federal executive orders issued over the course of 1942 permitted high-level commanders to establish security zones from which certain persons might be excluded, froze the assets of "enemy aliens" and imposed curfews on enemy aliens and Japanese Americans. General DeWitt took full advantage of these powers; his actions culminated in the Civilian Exclusion Order No. 34 of May 3, which forced all inhabitants of Japanese ancestry (as little as one-sixteenth) to report for assignment to internment camps in the interior for the duration of the war.

Pleasanton lay outside the high-priority exclusion zones (which primarily comprised the California coast) but fell within the second tier. Residents of Japanese ancestry were subject to curfew as of February 25, 1942, but were permitted to travel to and from work and for ordinary business purposes as long as they did not enter the "prohibited areas" to the west, while Japanese residents of said areas were forced to move (though they often could not afford to do so since their assets had been frozen).[275] Still, at the end of April, the Valley's Japanese and Japanese American residents were compelled to register for relocation, and on May 2 and 3, they were transported to an assembly center in Turlock; from there, they were sent to the Gila River internment camp in the desert southeast of Phoenix, Arizona.[276]

Due to the paucity of available sources, especially local newspapers, it is unfortunately difficult to tell much about how Pleasanton's non-Japanese residents viewed the matter. While there was considerable anger against the Japanese government in the wake of the Pearl Harbor attack, it is not clear how much of that anger was directed against locals of Japanese descent. Very few of the families who left in 1942 seem to have returned after 1945, but most of them had not owned property in the township before the war, and they may not have felt that they had much to come back to.

Homefront Mobilization

At the same time, the mobilization of personnel and resources left the Valley with a shortage of agricultural labor. The county mobilized

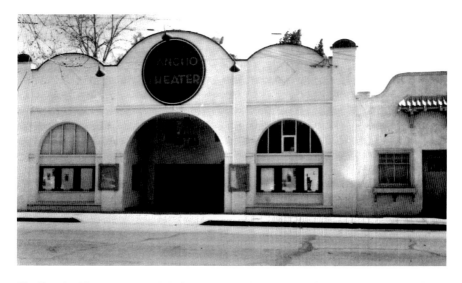

The Rancho Theater at 720 Main Street showed Spanish-language films to an audience largely composed of Mexican migrant workers, circa 1945. *Museum on Main.*

students and scoured the region for harvest labor, but even then, there were too few agricultural workers after industry and the armed forces had depleted the available labor force. The Roosevelt administration negotiated an agreement with the Mexican government to allow Mexican workers temporary visas to fill the need; several thousand of these laborers came to the Valley during the beet and tomato harvests, enough to support a Spanish-language movie theater on Main Street during their stay.[277] The high school provided evening English classes for the workers, and in one instance, a Spanish-speaking Pleasantonian was treated to an evening serenade after providing hospitality for a party of guest workers.[278]

The explosion of wartime economic activity, both military and civilian, put immense pressure on the Bay Area's housing stocks, and although it lay on the outskirts of the region, the Amador-Livermore Valley was no exception. Trailer parks provided temporary accommodations for some workers, a camp was set up on the fairgrounds for Mexican guest workers and still people put up in garages, residents' spare rooms, sheds and chicken coops—wherever a cot might be laid under a roof. The market responded when Harris Acres opened west of Third Street along Neal and Abbie; its fifty small family dwellings took some of the pressure off

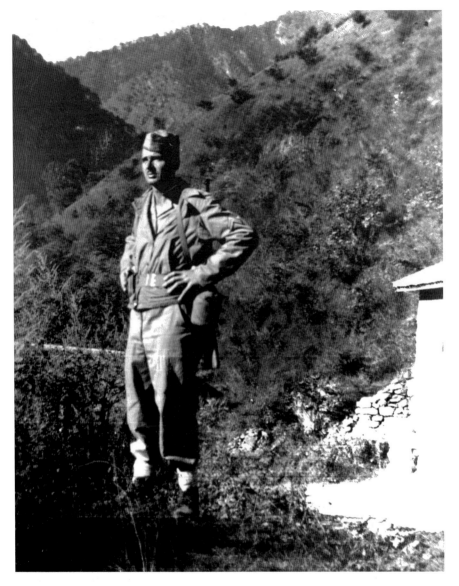

Pleasanton resident Jack Kolln (son of hardware merchant Herman Kolln) serving in China, 1945. *Museum on Main.*

Opposite: Pleasanton USO volunteers serve cake to naval personnel at the Veterans Memorial, 1945. *Museum on Main.*

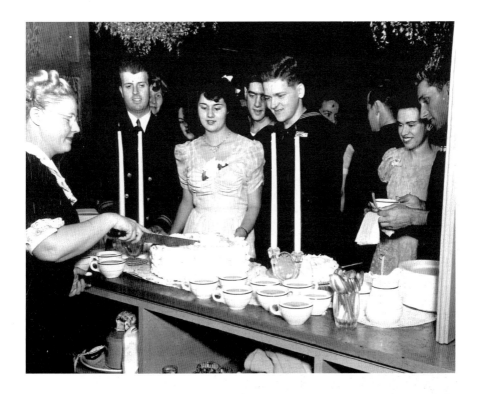

of the local housing market, but it was still stretched too tight.[279] The federal government stepped in, building a complex named Kottinger Village along Kottinger Avenue east of downtown and west of McKinley Park and another named Komandorski Village between Camp Parks and Dublin. Unlike Harris Acres, Kottinger Village was composed of two-story multi-family units and was even supplied with a communal cafeteria. Its residents and those of Komandorski were primarily civilian employees of the naval bases and families of military personnel stationed there long-term.

The mobilization of people and resources in Pleasanton, as in the rest of the country, exceeded even the high level set by the previous world war. By September 1943, more than 150 men from Pleasanton Township were already in service.[280] The city itself lost nine men as military casualties; the first of these was Ambrose Regalia, who died in a Japanese attack on Dutcher Harbor, Alaska, in June 1942.[281] On the homefront, people rolled up their sleeves for a routine of ration books, victory gardens, blood drives, scrap metal collections, renting spare rooms to war workers and hoping for good news from the battlefront.

The towns of the Valley formed local USO organizations to support the morale of the naval personnel at Parks, Shoemaker and the Livermore Air Station. They hosted receptions for the sailors and officers, giving up part of their sugar rations to bake cakes. They attended dances—although Pleasanton's young women earned some notoriety, according to one account, when they declined to attend a dance for the Seabees, who were older than the average naval recruit and usually drawn from the building trades.[282] (They apparently exhibited fewer reservations about entertaining the new recruits at Shoemaker.)

By the end of the war, the Valley had experienced a brief taste of rapid growth, even if wartime strictures prevented residents from enjoying its fruits. The region had bounced back from a great agricultural and business depression on the wave of wartime mobilization, and it had learned to accommodate more than ten thousand new inhabitants, if temporarily. It was clear that the region had great potential, but the question remained: how could it be realized once the war was over and its stimulus to the economy faded?

PART III
PLEASANTON GROWING

So This Is Growth, 1945–1970

After the euphoria of victory and homecoming had passed, the end of the war brought new uncertainty to Pleasanton and to the Valley in general. Once the wartime sailors had been successfully mustered out (which would be done by late 1946), the U.S. Navy would no longer need the Parks/Shoemaker complex, and a significant source of demand would be gone. After the last war, the Valley's population had dropped below the level of the last census; what would happen once the furnaces of victory no longer needed to be fed?

Through the early 1950s, a number of developments pointed the way to new growth and new directions for the Valley. First, the U.S. Air Force adopted Camp Parks as a basic training facility in 1951, bringing a new influx of military personnel into the Valley and a new source of demand for local business.[283] Much more significantly, in 1950, the Atomic Energy Commission took over the land on which the Livermore Naval Air Station had been built for the construction of a laboratory devoted to nuclear weapons research.[284] The Livermore Radiation Laboratory (later known as Lawrence Livermore National Laboratory, or LLNL) began operations in 1952 and grew much faster than anyone had expected, and although Livermore felt the brunt of its impact, some of the new scientists, engineers and bureaucrats made their homes in Pleasanton.

Soon afterward, General Electric built the nation's first private-sector nuclear facility at Vallecitos south of town; although it would never be as significant an employer as the lab, it nonetheless added about six hundred well-paid jobs to the economy of Pleasanton Township.[285]

Housing Boom Warmup: The 1950s

The early and mid-1950s thus brought a new round of growth and development to Pleasanton, a round that seemed rapid at the time but would prove to be only a warmup for the following decade. Most of the new residential construction lay to the east and northeast of the city's existing built-up area. Livermore real estate developer Roy Jensen built a small subdivision called Walnut Drive on the Arroyo del Valle, east of Main, in 1952; the same year, Allen and Riedeman built Amador Court, a 27-unit residential development off Vineyard Avenue, again to the northeast of downtown.[286] Three years later, Jensen built Pioneer Village, 211 units laid out north of the old city boundary, across Santa Rita Road from Amador Valley High School. This new subdivision, the largest built in Pleasanton up to that date, also provided the town with a second elementary school to serve the northern part of town; after a contest sponsored by the school district, it took the name Alisal Elementary School.[287] In 1960, it would be joined by Valley View Elementary, located off Kottinger Drive in the northeast part of town.

Much of the financial infrastructure for residential development came from New Deal legislation: the Federal Home Loan Bank Act of 1932, the establishment of the Federal Housing Administration in 1934 and the establishment of the Federal National Mortgage Association (later known as Fannie Mae) in 1938 were all designed to foster home ownership by making financing simpler, cheaper and more easily obtained.[288] Wartime mobilization helped build personal incomes while restricting consumption, leaving many people with savings that could serve as down payments after rationing ended. The growing highway system, not to mention increasingly affordable air travel, made moving about the country for work more feasible than ever before. All of these factors unleashed a major housing boom in the postwar era, and California was one of the places where the boom cracked the loudest.

All over town, the landscape seemed to be in flux. The Nevis Pavilion had been torn down during the war; its space became a used car lot.[289] In

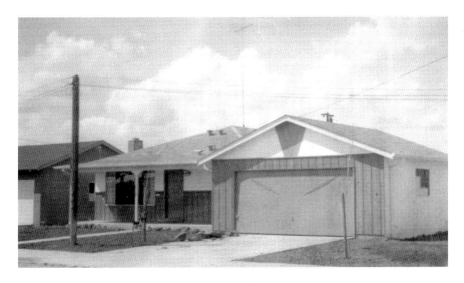

The Burt home on Jensen Street in Pioneer Village, circa 1956. Major Warren Burt, a pilot trainer at Parks Air Force Base, was one of the first purchasers in the development. *Museum on Main.*

1950, the fairgrounds initiated a program to convert its open-air display shed into a modern exhibition hall, and a drive-in theater opened north of the high school on Santa Rita Road.[290] The old grammar school on First and Abbie was deemed too small and unsafe; in its place rose a new school facility, finished in 1956, with separate wings for primary and middle-grade students. That same year, Bank of America bought the old Rose Hotel and razed it to build a new bank with a parking lot.[291]

The pace of growth, and its apparent lack of direction, alarmed a number of civic groups, and in April 1953, representatives from the Women's Improvement Club, the American Legion and the American Legion ladies' auxiliary formally requested that the city council adopt a zoning ordinance.[292] After some study and public input (as well as discussion of a few stopgaps such as tweaking the building code), the council approved a final draft in February 1954 by unanimous vote.[293]

The code divided all land within the city limits (as of October 1, 1953) into three zones: a residential zone, a commercial/business zone and a misnamed "unrestricted" zone designed to accommodate existing uses (including a small gravel business on St. John Street) while prohibiting industries deemed to pose health or safety hazards (such as glue factories, ore refineries or slaughterhouses). Residential uses were permitted in all three zones. The unrestricted zone comprised primarily the area from the west side of First

Street to the west side of Main, plus a section along the north side of St. John extending west to Pleasanton Avenue. The commercial zone lay just south of the St. John arm of the unrestricted zone, occupying a strip 150 feet wide between the back side of the Main Street properties and Pleasanton Avenue. The rest of town was zoned residential, a designation that also permitted home businesses without storefronts, both professional (such as doctors and attorneys) and otherwise (such as seamstresses). The ordinance also specified a minimum lot size of 5,000 square feet for new structures, although smaller lots with existing structures were grandfathered in.

Small-Town Culture in a Growing City

Despite the doubling of the city's population over the course of the 1950s and '60s, Pleasanton retained much of its tightknit, small-town character. Local events—such as parades, high school sports and theatricals, as well as benefit events such as the Fireman's Ball—played a significant role in the culture of the community. Parades to celebrate Independence Day, Halloween and the Alameda County Fair brought residents and

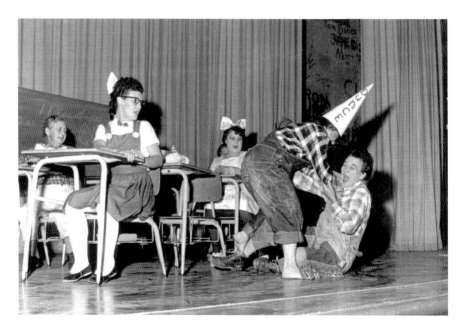

A classroom sketch from the 1963 Scholarship Frolics. *Museum on Main.*

visitors to Main Street annually, and the fair parade was always one of the highlights of the year. The Scholarship Frolics, a benefit revue to help Amador graduates train for the teaching profession, drew enthusiastic audiences during its annual performances from 1953 to 1963.[294] The Frolics drew in participants not only from school faculty and staff but also from many of Pleasanton's adult organizations and clubs.

The College that Wasn't

As the state's population and economy grew, demand for higher education grew along with it. In 1955, southern Alameda County joined the regions where the state legislature sought to establish a new campus in the State College system. Two cities emerged as the strongest candidates to host it: Hayward and Pleasanton.[295] Although the administrations at University of California and San Jose State College were opposed to creating a local rival

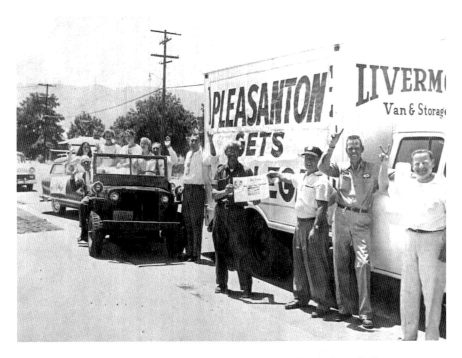

Residents celebrate the (premature) announcement of a California State College campus awarded to Pleasanton, 1959. *Museum on Main.*

for tuition dollars, plans inched forward over the next three years. By June 1959, Pleasanton seemed to have the prize all but won. The Orloff family were prepared to sell a significant portion of their farmland north of town, and residents of Pleasanton rejoiced in the streets.[296] However, the struggle only seemed to be over. Hayward politicians, led by Assemblyman Carlos Bee, managed to reopen the question, and by the end of the year, the state had accepted their offer of the 345-acre former Hauschildt property in the Hayward hills. Pleasanton and Livermore locals chalked the result up to the more populous city's greater political clout.

Annexation Race: Pleasanton and the Valley Community Services District

Pleasanton's growth might have maintained this relatively leisurely pace were it not for the appearance of an external factor. Almost since the end of the war, developers had hoped for the opportunity to leverage the water and sewage infrastructure installed by the navy during World War II. In 1953, some landowners in the area founded the Parks Community Service District under a 1951 state law providing for the organization of public services in unincorporated areas, with the hopes of negotiating access to the base's water and sewer lines.[297]

The plan went nowhere, but the district was still recognized by the state in 1959 when Los Angeles developers Kenneth Volk and Robert McLain announced plans to build a primarily residential development on more than four thousand acres around the junction of Highway 50 and State Route 21. Stretching across the Alameda–Contra Costa county line, the proposed San Ramon Village would add as many as thirteen thousand dwellings to the upper Amador Valley, with some land set aside for commercial and industrial development. With the county planning department coordinating the decision-making process and various stakeholders (including the Cities of Pleasanton and Livermore) involved, the Volk-McLain proposal was adopted.[298]

In order to ensure services for this new community in unincorporated lands—especially the potentially troublesome questions of water and sewer services—the Volk-McLain firm underwrote a reorganization of the Parks Community Service District. Renamed the Valley Community Services District (VCSD), this new entity assumed responsibility not only for water and sewage (with infrastructure improvements financed by Volk-McLain) but also fire protection, parks and garbage collection in the unincorporated Dublin–San Ramon area. With further expansion in mind, Volk-McLain made sure that VCSD's water delivery and sewage treatment systems not only could cope with the needs of the developments it had already planned but could also be easily upgraded to serve an even broader population.[299]

Construction of San Ramon Village began in the summer of 1960, with the first residents moved in by November. Under Alameda County's zoning laws, less restrictive than Contra Costa's, the Dublin portion of the development quickly filled up with smaller, more affordable houses and strip-style commercial zones—hardly the "next Piedmont" that boosters such as *Times* publisher John Edmands had in mind for Pleasanton, or even what the authors of the 1958 General Plan had intended in their less exclusive (but still mid-market) zoning arrangements.[300] Pleasantonians looked nervously at the township map and saw Volk-McLain's interests extending south of Highway 50, including not only the floodplain of the former hop fields (and the Hansen-Geiger dairy) but also down along the foothills west of town.

To ensure a greater say over the development of these lands, which the city had long considered part of its natural sphere of influence, Pleasanton embarked on the most sweeping round of land annexations in its history. During the years between 1954 and 1960, the city had annexed 186 acres of property.[301] From 1960 through 1963, however, Pleasanton filed for a further 790 acres to be brought within the city limits, much of it in the expanded VCSD service area. In this endeavor, it had support from two developers with significant holdings southwest of what would become the 580/680 junction: Stoneson Development Corporation and Schulte-Blackwell.[302]

Pleasanton's annexation plans did not go unchallenged. In early 1963, a group led by Alameda County deputy sheriff Lawrence Wilson, a reputed Volk-McLain ally, filed a petition for incorporating Dublin within boundaries that stretched south of I-580 to encompass land that Pleasanton had already moved to annex.[303] The ensuing legal and administrative battle took nearly three years to settle and went all the way to the California Supreme Court, where Pleasanton won the case on the grounds that its annexation motions had been filed first. Another arena of conflict between VCSD and Pleasanton was the Alameda County Local Agency Formation Commission (LAFCO), a state-mandated body tasked with overseeing the establishment of governmental entities so as to prevent conflicts of jurisdiction and ensure orderly growth and development. Here Pleasanton's status as an incorporated city gave it an advantage over VCSD, and over the course of 1964, the city annexed more than 1,100 acres. However, in

December 1966, after Pleasanton filed to annex 2,100 acres of industrial land along I-580 between I-680 and Santa Rita Road, the Alameda County LAFCO stepped in with a proposal to end the ongoing land battles: annex Dublin to Pleasanton and be done with it.[304]

The proposal appealed to many Pleasanton residents, but the measure required approval from both communities, and Dubliners were more skeptical—especially after Pleasanton announced that it would build its new civic center on Bernal Avenue, at the opposite end of town from Dublin. In addition, Pleasanton's continuing attempts to annex land in the area south of I-580 struck many Dublin residents as unwarranted land-grabbing. When the measure reached the ballot in June 1967, Pleasanton voters approved it by a comfortable margin, but Dublin voters rejected it by more than three to one, with 59 percent of them turning out—in an off-year election, no less—to express their displeasure.[305] Dublin remained separate and would eventually incorporate in 1982.

Bigger Boom: Residential Development in the 1960s

Despite this setback, Pleasanton was able by the end of the decade to bring most of the land south of I-580 within its city limits. Between 1960 and 1971, in fact, Pleasanton increased its acreage by about 700 percent, and much of that new land would end up slated for residential development. Relying on VCSD for water and sewage services in much of the new territory (despite the bad blood between the city and the service district), Pleasanton extended permits for several new housing developments in the annexed lands. The city, realizing that its original general plan had not accounted for the pace of annexation or for the increase in demand for development, commissioned a thorough revision in 1965.[306] The new plan covered an area of nearly forty-four square miles—for its future, the city expressed ambitions for a community of distinctive character, growing in a balanced fashion to maintain a high quality of life for a spectrum of income groups. As part of this vision, the plan also foresaw Pleasanton as the location for a regional shopping center to serve the entire Valley, as well as the preservation of downtown Pleasanton's unique character and its continued importance to the local economy—although not necessarily as a shopping district.

However, it turned out that residential development was much easier to attract than clean industrial or non-strip commercial development. Six subdivisions were already under construction when the 1965 general

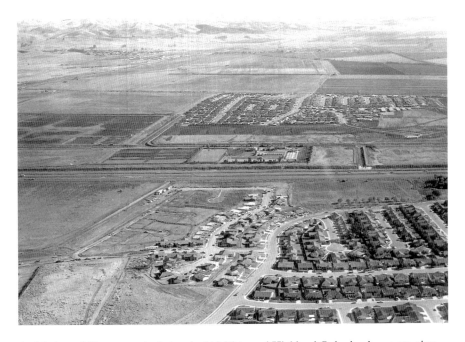

Aerial view of Pleasanton depicting the Val-Vista and Highland Oaks developments, circa 1970. Val-Vista is in the center background, while Highland Oaks is in the right foreground. *Museum on Main.*

plan took effect; as the decade wore on, more and more new tract plans would be filed with the county recorder's office. Concerns over the spread of "cheap" housing led to more restrictive zoning; in 1964, Livermore Lab engineer John Long was elected to the Pleasanton City Council (and selected as mayor) on a platform of "higher standards and lower density."[307] In 1968, a revised zoning ordinance raised minimum lot sizes for most residential land; a few higher-density projects were approved, but these still favored single-family dwellings. Proposals to construct apartment complexes met with considerable opposition from nearby residents. A proposal to revise the zoning laws to permit a mix of lot sizes with a higher average went nowhere.[308]

The Interstates

Although the 1956 federal highway act established that Highway 50 and State Route 21 would be upgraded as part of the interstate system, the

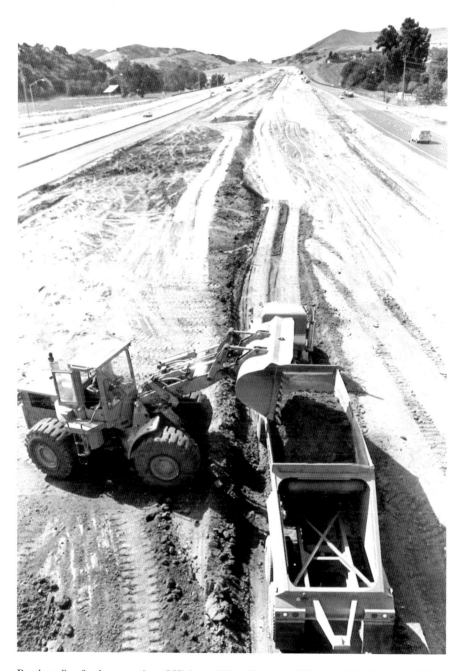
Road grading for the expansion of Highway 50 into Interstate 580, circa 1965. *Museum on Main.*

work of making those routes into freeways with on- and off-ramps did not begin until 1963.[309] Ten to fifteen miles at a time, sections were widened and repaved, interchanges constructed and overpasses built. By 1967, the work was complete: Interstate 580 crossed the Amador-Livermore Valley from east to west, linking the Central Valley with the Bay, and Interstate 680 ran north–south through the Valley's western end, completing an artery that ran from San Jose northward across the Carquinez Strait. Travel between the Amador-Livermore Valley and the rest of the state had never been easier. Unfortunately, the state highway authority neglected to name Pleasanton on the Bernal Avenue exit signage—or on any of the other signs, for that matter—and the city had to petition Sacramento for the oversight to be rectified.[310]

A Slowly Expanding Job Base

Much of the residential development ended up housing commuters who worked outside the Valley (and, to a lesser extent, in Livermore), but development also brought jobs into the Pleasanton area—albeit not nearly as many jobs as new residents. The road to Sunol, south of central Pleasanton, was perhaps the most noteworthy site for this expansion, as first Harper & Row and then Scholastic Magazines, and then D.C. Heath as well, built distribution facilities along what became known as "publishers' row" between 1963 and 1965. In 1964, Kaiser Aluminum announced that it would build a research center in the area; the new Kaiser Technology Center was completed in 1969.[311] In the same year, Volkswagen built a distribution facility at the interchange of I-580 and I-680.[312]

Less welcome, in the end, was a plan announced in 1968 by the owners of Arlington's Six Flags Over Texas to build an amusement park on the site of the Meadowlark Dairy near the western foothills. Rising land prices and looming tax increases had convinced the Takens family (who had leased and then purchased the dairy from the Briggs family) to shift the dairy's herds and operations to Tracy on the other side of the Altamont Pass. Initial enthusiasm for the project waned once prospective neighbors began to consider the noise and traffic that an amusement park would bring. Furthermore, the developers seemed uninterested in the city's request for other types of industry to supplement the park. Less than a year after the initial proposal, Great Southwest Corporation

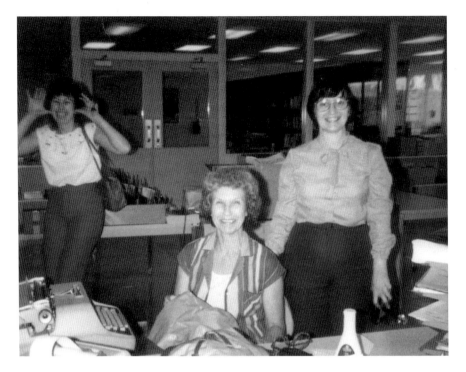

Scholastic Magazines staff at the Sunol Boulevard distribution center, 1970s. *Museum on Main.*

cancelled the project—although financial difficulties rather than local opposition may have been the primary reason for its demise.[313]

Updating Government

As Pleasanton's area and population swelled during this period, it threatened to outgrow the small-town government that had administered it during the first half of the century. Certainly the municipal payroll had added a few positions before World War II, but Pleasanton's population doubled between 1940 and 1950, nearly doubled again between 1950 and 1960 and then more than tripled by 1970, when the census recorded more than eighteen thousand residents. In 1956, the position of city administrative officer was created, later to become city manager.[314] In 1964, the fire department hired its first full-time firefighters, beginning the gradual transition to an all-professional force.[315] The police department,

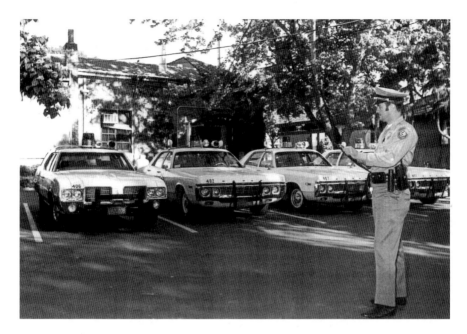

Officer inspecting Pleasanton police cars behind city hall, circa 1970. *Museum on Main.*

which numbered four sworn officers as late as 1954, grew to thirteen full-time employees (including eight sworn officers) by 1964. The public works department, which had begun with a single engineer in about 1900, expanded to encompass twenty employees in five separate divisions; the infant parks department was represented on the payroll by one full-time recreation coordinator. These paid servants of the community were also backed up by volunteer commissions, including a planning commission and a commission for parks and recreation.

The little town hall on Main Street could no longer contain all of these growing functions. The library was the first to go; it moved up and across the street in 1962 and then to a location on Bernal Avenue in 1968.[316] Other city functions were spun off to annexed offices around the corner on Division Street. In 1965, the city council itself began meeting at the Women's Improvement Club facility, formerly the Kottinger Village cafeteria and community center.[317] The need for a newer, larger city hall was clear, but it would have to wait until the following decade.

Water, Waste and Growth

As always, concerns over water and sewage accompanied growth. Pleasanton had turned down an opportunity to participate in the Hetch Hetchy water system during the Depression, trusting instead in its own ground water resources and its earlier arrangements with Spring Valley—since bought out by the City of San Francisco. Unfortunately, the local aquifers began to run low again in the early 1950s, and local authorities once again cast about for a solution.

A 1953 proposal to form a water and flood-control district covering Washington, Pleasanton and Murray Townships was rejected by Murray and Pleasanton voters over concerns that most of the benefits would accrue to Washington Township.[318] A similar plan for only the Valley found a more sympathetic audience, especially after historic floods in December of 1955, and the Zone 7 water district was duly established in 1957. In 1960, a statewide initiative authorized more than $5 million in bonds for improving water supply and flood control; Zone 7 became the conduit for the Valley's share of these improvements. Flood control would be of particular importance for Pleasanton's future growth because the land north of town—formerly the hop fields and before that dominated by the Laguna—was especially prone to flooding, which tended to discourage potential developers. However, Pleasanton opted out of purchasing its water through Zone 7 for the next decade, firm in the belief that its existing arrangements with San Francisco would remain sufficient.[319]

While the water district handled flood control and the city relied on its existing sources of water supply, management of Pleasanton's waste water became divided between the city's own increasingly obsolete treatment plant, which served central Pleasanton and neighborhoods to its east and south, and the newer, larger-capacity system managed by VCSD, which served the northern and western developments annexed by Pleasanton during the 1960s. The district had upgraded and expanded its treatment plant in 1960, and both Pleasanton and VCSD agreed in principle that the best solution would be to have VCSD take over all of Pleasanton's sewage treatment. However, resentments from the struggle over the lands between Pleasanton and Dublin hampered cooperation; agreement to serve north and west Pleasanton was only reached in 1967, and as the 1960s ended, the old Pleasanton treatment plant was still in service.[320]

Preserving the Past:
The Amador-Livermore Valley Historical Society

It was in this context of accelerating development, with a rapidly changing landscape and a large influx of new residents from outside the Valley (not to mention growing conflicts over the direction of its development), that the Amador-Livermore Valley Historical Society was born.[321] Founding members included scions of old Valley families such as Herb Hagemann (a direct descendant of John Kottinger), William Apperson (Phoebe Hearst's great-grandnephew), Mildred Clark (another Bernal descendant) and Evelyn Moller (whose husband's family came to Pleasanton in 1910), as well as history-loving newcomers such as Justi Rogers, the society's first president, and Reginald Stuart, who came to the Valley in about 1960 after careers as an Oakland high school teacher and successful realtor. The society's first programs involved organizing

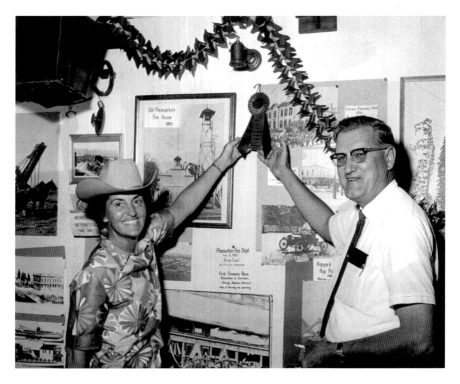

ALVHS members Marie Cronin and Herb Hagemann show off the society's exhibit at the Alameda County Fair, circa 1968. *Museum on Main.*

lectures and supporting research and publication in the early history of the area, in particular the period of the ranchos and of the foundation of the Valley's towns. In 1965, the group undertook its first preservation project when it acquired the old St. Raymond's Catholic Church in Dublin. (In 1993, the society would sell the building to the City of Dublin.) In 1970, the society established a museum on the Alameda County Fairgrounds to showcase its mission and collections.[322]

Living in the Atomic Valley

By the end of the 1950s, the Amador-Livermore Valley had become established as a center for both civilian and military nuclear research, with GE's Vallecitos facility at the west end and LLNL at the east. Experts (including Manhattan Project veteran and lab cofounder Edward Teller) had tried to allay any worries about having nuclear facilities nearby, and serving as home to such cutting-edge projects could be as much a source of pride as of concern.[323] The county fair adopted a mascot named

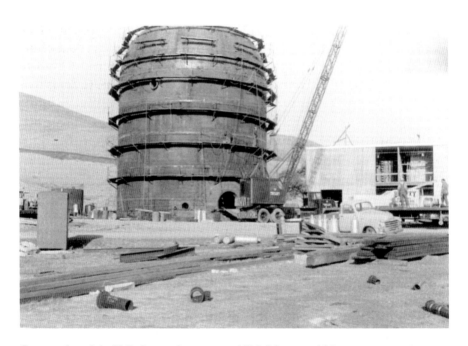

Construction of the Vallecitos nuclear reactor, 1956. *Museum on Main.*

"Atomic Al," and *Times* publisher John Edmands provided a glowing report of the Vallecitos plant's benefits for a nationally distributed *New York Times* supplement sponsored by General Electric.[324]

At the same time, the presence of a nuclear research facility in the Valley gave an extra edge to Cold War fears, for it made the Valley an even more valuable target for Soviet missiles than the air force base did. Civil defense planning against nuclear attack began at the county level in 1950, with local coordinators assigned to organize preparations for a response.[325] Air raid drills became a regular feature of school life for a few years; some residents even constructed fallout shelters. After the Korean War, the program fell into neglect in Pleasanton (as opposed to in Livermore, where the proximity of the lab called for greater caution), until the Berlin crisis of 1961 prompted the city to revive civil defense measures for a brief time.[326]

The Castlewood Fire

In 1952, the Marshalls sold Old Hearst Ranch to a group that planned to turn the dude ranch resort back into a country club, with the former Hearst mansion again serving as its clubhouse.[327] The new Castlewood Country Club hosted everything from golf tournaments to high school proms on the historic grounds. On the night of August 24, 1969, a fire began in one of the unoccupied wings of the clubhouse; faulty wiring was later blamed.[328] Without an up-to-date alarm or sprinkler system, the fire had grown to dangerous proportions by the time anyone detected it and called for help. Eventually, ten different firefighting agencies took part in containing the blaze, with ninety-two firefighters supported by thirty pieces of major equipment. However, the local water supply was insufficient to put out the fire on its own, and despite draining Castlewood's 200,000-gallon swimming pool, firefighters still had to send tankers back to Pleasanton for extra water. In the end, the fire was prevented from spreading beyond the clubhouse, but the historic residence could not be saved. The country club would open a new clubhouse in a similar style on the site of the Hacienda within a few years.

The Castlewood fire might be seen as symbolic of an era's end: one of the great landmarks of the old Amador Valley laid low as the region's population swelled and its economy and politics modernized. But it would be too much to say that Pleasanton swept the old away to make room for the new, even in the rapid development of the 1960s. Although the city had not yet made a firm commitment to historic preservation, there

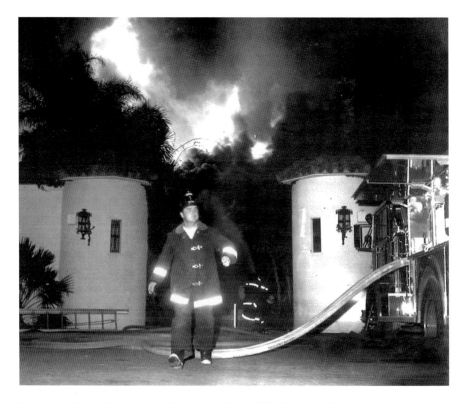

Firefighter Larry Howard at the Castlewood fire, 1969. *Museum on Main.*

was still considerable sentiment in favor of maintaining an attractive and vibrant downtown without wholesale renovation. The foundation of a historical society demonstrated that at least part of the community wished to ensure that the Valley's past would not be plowed under. And when events at the beginning of the 1970s forced a pause in the pace of change, there would come greater opportunities to reconsider the relationship between the new Pleasanton and the old one.

CRISIS AND RENEWAL, 1970–1990

As the 1970s began, concerns about the rapid growth of the Valley came to dominate local politics. At a time when environmental and demographic issues became prominent in the national discourse, the Amador-Livermore Valley experienced heavy air pollution, an insecure water supply and an overburdened wastewater treatment system. Many residents feared that the quality of life for which they had come would disappear if no action were taken to control development—in particular, residential development. In Pleasanton, water and wastewater issues would impose an unavoidable curb through much of the 1970s; however, after those challenges were resolved, the politics of development would assert themselves as Pleasanton continued to leave its agricultural origins behind.

Water Politics

The Zone 7 management had struck a major blow for flood control in 1969 with the completion of the Del Valle Dam, which controlled the flow of the Arroyo del Valle at a point about ten miles south of Livermore and created a reservoir that would also serve as a recreational lake.[329] However, water supply issues once again hovered over the horizon, especially in Pleasanton, where continued reliance on the "surplus waters of the Alameda Creek" guarantee in the city's water rights had seriously depleted local aquifers once again. In order to deal with this problem (and with Livermore's issues regarding water supplies and wastewater treatment), Zone 7 proposed Project Two, which in addition to expanding Livermore's treatment capacity and better connecting it with Valley water systems would have built a pipeline connecting Pleasanton to the state water project, thereby not only securing water supplies for the foreseeable future but also recharging the depleted groundwater of the western Valley. The measure failed in 1969 because the small property tax hike that funded it offended the prevailing belief that "growth should pay for itself." A revised version, replacing the tax increase with hookup fees, passed easily in 1972.

The "Million-Gallon" Wastewater Incident

In late July 1971, staff at VCSD's wastewater treatment plant detected and repaired a leaking air hose. They quickly discovered that the air leak had disguised the actual amount of sewage being processed by the system; instead of operating at a little under capacity, it was operating at about 125 percent of capacity, pushing between 500,000 and 750,000 gallons more wastewater through the system than VCSD had believed it was processing.[330]

Even before the "million-gallon" incident, county and state water authorities had been concerned about wastewater treatment in the Pleasanton/VCSD area. Because the VCSD and Pleasanton water treatment systems eventually emptied into the Niles Cone groundwater basin, from which Washington Township drew much of its water, the Regional Water Quality Control Board already kept a close eye on Pleasanton wastewater, holding it to some of the highest standards in the state. VCSD management realized that drastic measures were needed; in early September, it declared a moratorium on new sewer hookups until the problem was resolved.[331]

The moratorium left Pleasanton in an unenviable position. At the time it was declared, the city council had made several commitments to residential developments that had not yet been built. And Pleasanton's own wastewater treatment plant had become the target of resident complaints about unpleasant odors.[332] Neither authority was in an immediate position to expand treatment capacity; for the time being, Pleasanton's era of rapid growth had come to an abrupt halt.

The Slow-Growth Movement and the SAVE Initiative

The sewer moratorium came at a time of growing controversy over development in the Valley. Concern over water issues, air pollution, traffic and suburban sprawl motivated a group of Valley residents to demand a more restrictive approach. The immediate spark in Pleasanton was a backlash against an apartment/condominium complex on Foothill Road near Castlewood Country Club, for which the city council had granted a zoning change to approve the more intensive use. Nearby residents fought back to prevent what they saw as the despoliation of a scenic byway. The "Rural Foothill Defenders" won an initiative campaign to repeal the zoning decision; in the wake of this victory, growth-control proponents decided it was time to apply the lessons of the Castlewood campaign to the entire Valley.

On October 16, 1971, an organization called Save All Valley Environments (SAVE) announced its existence. SAVE attracted members from both Pleasanton and Livermore, although its primary constituency seems to have been residents who had arrived since the establishment of the Livermore Lab. Many of its active members had been involved in attempts to convince the administrations of Pleasanton and Livermore to slow the pace of growth, and their frustration with the existing machinery of government led them to try the initiative process.[333]

SAVE's initiative measure, submitted for separate votes in Pleasanton and Livermore, would establish a growth-control ordinance in each city that prohibited new developments without "satisfactory solutions" to the burden they would impose on the Valley's water resources, sewage systems and schools. In this campaign, the group was backed by the *Independent*, a Livermore-based newspaper established in 1963 as a counterweight to the more old-resident, boosterist *Herald* and *Times* (both of which opposed the measure). In spite of vehement opposition from developers, larger landowners, realtors and the construction industry, the SAVE initiative passed in both Livermore and Pleasanton. The battle then moved from the voting booth to the courts.[334]

While the lawsuits over the SAVE ordinance worked their way through the legal system, the city attempted to deal with its existing commitments. Although the Pleasanton City Council had decided not to join Livermore's appeal after a Superior Court judge overturned the law, the sewer hookup moratorium still imposed an unavoidable limit on new construction, and developers with money tied up in projects were becoming increasingly nervous. Twelve of them sued both the city and VCSD for $53 million in November 1971.[335] VCSD had received state funding for an expansion of its treatment facilities, but the work would not be complete until at least 1973. An out-of-court settlement established a temporary solution by which developers were assigned priority to receive new hookups as they became available, but for the long term, a more comprehensive approach would be necessary.[336]

LAVWMA: A New Water Solution

Competing jurisdictions, and the interests they served, were the most significant obstacle to solving the Valley's water problems. Although Zone 7 would have been a logical choice to manage both water supply and sewage treatment, as an Alameda County agency it excluded part of VCSD's service area; some residents in both Dublin and Pleasanton

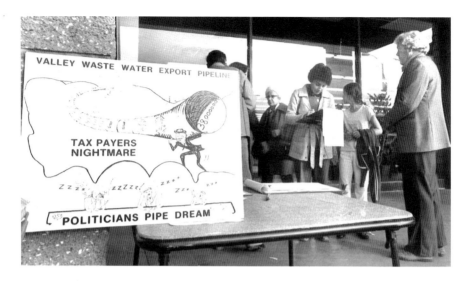

Volunteers gather signatures for a petition against the LAVWMA pipeline, circa 1976. *Museum on Main.*

worried that Zone 7 would subordinate their interests to those of large landowners in unincorporated areas. In 1974, all three were accommodated by a joint powers agreement forming a Livermore-Amador Valley Water Management Agency (LAVWMA), with two representatives each from Pleasanton, VCSD and Zone 7. By the end of the year, the new agency had developed a pipeline plan that would send treated wastewater out of the Valley and into a broader East Bay discharge system that emptied into the San Francisco Bay. However, opposition from residents concerned that the project would stimulate further residential development and contribute to increased air pollution delayed implementation until 1978.[337]

Keeping Downtown Vibrant

Spurred in part by a chamber of commerce in which downtown businesses were heavily represented, city planning made special efforts to nurture the downtown business district as Pleasanton's economic center even while commercial and office developments sprang up in the annexed areas north of the old town center. In 1974, the council proposed to create a special redevelopment zone encompassing the

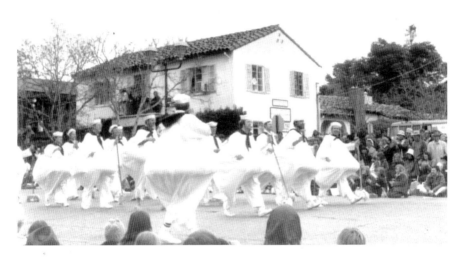

The Balloon Platoon, a favorite of Pleasanton parades from the 1970s onward, marches in the 1975 KNBR Good Times Parade. *Museum on Main.*

downtown business district, managed by an agency with broad powers to combat blight and pursue beautification projects. The plan was vehemently opposed by a group of activists known as Citizens Against Redevelopment, which worried about the concentration of power the redevelopment agency would represent.[338] With a few of the district's more influential businessmen also opposed, the idea died within a year.

The desire to revitalize the downtown district never completely disappeared, however; by 1978, the city's growth management plan called for establishing it as "a regional tourist/cultural center composed primarily of specialty stores, antique shops, unique restaurants, and entertainment activities all drawing on Pleasanton's unique cultural heritage."[339] This was a far cry from the utilitarian market center the district had been from the early days through the 1950s. In 1984, the city did establish a special downtown business district that worked through the local merchants' association (Pleasanton Downtown Association) to set and maintain standards for preserving downtown's distinctive historic character and aesthetic appeal.

Throughout the 1970s and '80s, downtown still remained the primary focus for any big event not hosted at the fairgrounds. From 1969 to 1975, it was the site of an annual, old-fashioned firemen's muster featuring skills competitions and vintage firefighting equipment. A Rotary-organized

"Heritage Days" street fair became an annual downtown event by the late 1970s. The by-now traditional parade previewing the county fair still marched down Main Street every year, and for a few years in mid-decade, it was joined by the KNBR Good Times Parade, which was organized as the result of a bet between two San Francisco disc jockeys. Of course, downtown was also the primary site for the city's celebration of the national bicentennial in 1976.

During the 1970s and 1980s, city government completed its move to the southern edge of the downtown district. The opening of the Pleasanton Civic Center as a new city hall in 1974 left only the police department in the old town hall by the arch, and by 1982 even the police had moved to a new facility on Bernal Avenue near the Civic Center. With the support of several organizations, including the association of downtown merchants, the historical society requested the use of the building as its museum, with the intention of leaving the fairgrounds for this more visible and accessible location.[340]

Catching Up: More Schools, More Services

As the city's population continued to grow, especially in 1971 and 1972 before the sewer hookup freeze delayed further home construction, demand for schools and other community services required an expansion of facilities. In 1968, Pleasanton received a new middle school (Harvest Park) and another elementary school (Walnut Grove); by 1975, the district had added two more elementary schools (Fairlands and Vintage Hills), and in 1973, the high school district built a second Pleasanton high school on the east side of, and named after, Foothill Road.[341]

As the need for classroom space drove the establishment of new schools, the growing number of families created demand for more parks. Providing park space had been an important feature of many of the new developments; in addition to these neighborhood parks, the city undertook to develop larger recreational projects. The first of these was an aquatic center with attached park along Black Avenue, north of Amador High, dedicated in 1970. The following year, the U.S. Department of the Interior gave the city a 105-acre parcel east of Hopyard Road, between the Arroyo Mocho and the Pleasanton Canal, for parkland; the city turned it into a dedicated sports park, building several baseball, softball

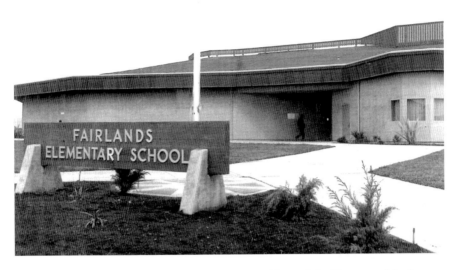

Fairlands Elementary School, built in 1973 to serve residents of the Pleasanton Meadows development. *Museum on Main.*

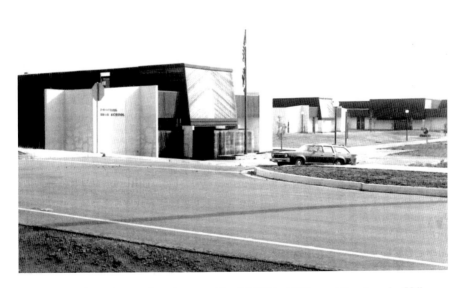

Foothill High School opened on the west side of I-680 in 1973, providing Amador Valley High with a crosstown rival. *Museum on Main.*

and soccer fields, as well as spectator and playground facilities, over the next two decades.

The public library, maintained by the county library system, also outgrew its walls. In 1973, it left the portable on Bernal Avenue for a larger, more permanent building on Black Avenue near the aquatic center. This facility remained its home for only fifteen years, however; in 1988, the library would move to yet another new building, this time next door to the Civic Center.

The rapid spread of residential developments over the 1960s and early 1970s also put extra stress on the fire department, although improved construction methods, more fire-resistant materials and improved fire prevention education meant that its firefighting role was increasingly subordinate to its role as paramedics and first responders. The number of full-time firefighters rose, and the volunteers were held to a higher standard of training even as their part diminished. In 1967, the city had issued bonds to finance the construction of three new stations; in the meantime, a temporary second station was established west of I-680 in the Fairland Oaks development. By 1972, a third station on Santa Rita Road was operational, and a permanent Stoneridge station was established during the construction of Hacienda Business Park in the early 1980s.

Ohlone Renaissance

As the civil rights movement spread beyond addressing segregation to embrace activism for a wider range of social-justice goals, descendants of East Bay Ohlone tribes, including those who traced their families back to the Alisal Ranchería, were inspired to reorganize in order to recover, preserve and protect their heritage. With support from the American Indian Historical Society, members of this group incorporated as a tribal organization in 1971 for the purpose of overseeing the Ohlone cemetery at Mission Dolores and representing the tribe when construction or other projects involved Ohlone cultural resources, such as grave sites or other archaeological finds. From this work, it was a short step to seeking federal recognition; for various reasons (including intra-tribal politics), a different organization, the Muwekma Ohlone Tribal Council, was established in the early 1980s and took up the task of petitioning the Bureau of Indian Affairs for recognition.[342]

Stoneridge Mall

In 1972, planning began for the regional shopping center that Pleasanton had sought to attract since the middle of the previous decade. Stoneson Development Corporation reached an agreement with the city to build the center on a site southwest of the 580/680 interchange. Because it was predominantly a commercial project, Stoneridge Shopping Center did not attract the same sort of opposition that many of the residential developments did, despite concerns about traffic. However, the complicated nature of the project, and the number of stakeholders involved, meant that ground would not be broken for construction until 1978. The final result, opening in the fall of 1980, was an enclosed mall of the type that had become typical of larger California shopping centers during the 1970s, with large anchor stores connected by broad halls on which smaller shops, restaurants and offices opened. The original anchors were Emporium, Macy's and J.C. Penney; a fourth anchor store, from the high-end Nordstrom chain, joined them in 1990.[343]

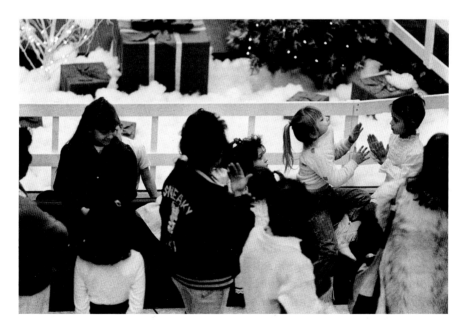

The last shopping day before Christmas at Stoneridge Mall, 1987. *Museum on Main/Bay Area News Group.*

Office Space: The New Boom

The growth of middle-management and other white-collar jobs in the 1960s and 1970s put a lot of pressure on the market for office space in the San Francisco area, and by the end of the 1970s, many companies were looking for less expensive yet still convenient places for subsidiary and divisional offices. This search provided Pleasanton with the job-creating opportunity the city had hoped for since the 1960s. The first major project along these lines was an eighty-two-acre office center on Hopyard Road, originally featuring high-rises of up to fourteen stories but scaled down to three five-story buildings when the city council responded to resident concerns by imposing a sixty-five-foot height limit. The Meyer project was approved by referendum in November 1981.[344]

More controversial would be a project to develop a business park encompassing nearly one thousand acres, to be developed in two phases, on the property along I-580 between Hopyard Road and Santa Rita Road, adjacent to the much smaller Meyer development. Although developers

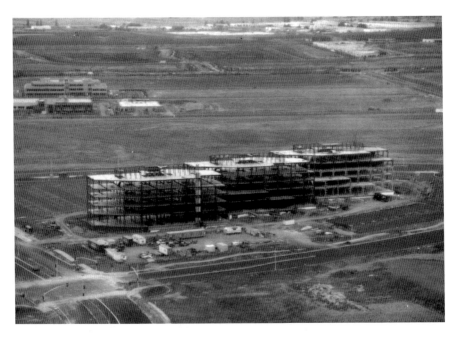

The three buildings of Hacienda Center (later Hacienda Terrace) were among the first completed in Hacienda Business Park and opened for tenants in 1984. *Museum on Main.*

Callahan-Pentz and Prudential Insurance worked closely with city planners and included flood control, traffic management, a mass-transit system and all utilities in its development plan, the sheer size of the project caused grave concerns for some residents—many worried that it would completely change the character of the community. Others saw it as an irresistible opportunity to complete a transformation underway since the 1950s on terms highly favorable to Pleasanton. The council approved Hacienda Business Park unanimously in June 1982, and opponents sought other avenues to halt it or force its scaling down.[345]

Most of the opposition coalesced into an organization called Citizens for Balanced Growth (CBG). Alleging that the city council had violated the terms of its general plan in approving Hacienda and that the environmental impact review had been inadequate, CBG sued the city. A Superior Court judge ruled against the city but did not halt the construction currently underway, providing an opportunity for the council to amend the general plan accordingly. CBG then gathered signatures to force a referendum, and a variety of citizens' and other groups arrayed on both sides of the issue. The referendum was held in April 1984, and Hacienda proponents (who had spent significant sums on the campaign) carried the voting by a three-to-two margin.

More Housing

The flurry of office construction in the early 1980s tipped the balance between housing and jobs in the opposite direction from the housing-dominated 1960s. With water and sewage issues settled for the immediate future and tightened emissions standards bringing air pollution under control, the externally imposed restrictions of the 1970s were relaxed, making new housing developments more viable and stimulating demand. However, the statewide passage of Proposition 13 in 1978 put strict limits on property tax hikes, making new housing less attractive to cities that depended on property tax revenues to fund the schools and municipal services that both existing and future residents would use.[346] Put simply, new residents threatened to cost more in services than they would pay in taxes. In addition, new housing developments in the 1980s were often proposed for tracts that lay in between earlier developments, and their prospective neighbors feared that increased traffic, spoiled views and similar inconveniences would affect their quality of life and property values. Multi-family units in particular tended to arouse opposition; in addition to the aforementioned concerns, residents cited threats to privacy (due to nearby two-story buildings potentially overlooking their backyards) and even increased crime as the likely results of bringing apartment complexes into their neighborhoods. Nonetheless, during the first half of the 1980s, the city managed largely to meet its plan goals for broadening diversity of housing and saw several projects for apartment, condominium and townhouse development to completion.[347]

By the end of the 1980s, Pleasanton had essentially completed its transformation from a rural market town to a modern suburban city. Although there was still some open land in the edges of the western Valley, and though old ranching families such as the Koopmanns and Spotornos were able to maintain some pasturage around Sunol and southern Pleasanton, development and annexation had stretched Pleasanton's boundaries from the western foothills to the valley center and from Interstate 580 south to Happy Valley. Agriculture had been almost entirely displaced in the local economy by white-collar corporate work, wholesale and retail distribution, light industry and, of course, real estate development. There was still room available to grow, but an increasing number of residents had begun to wonder whether growth had reached an appropriate limit. Development issues would continue to play a significant role in city (and regional) politics for the coming decades into the twenty-first century.

Into the Twenty-first Century

Since the end of the 1980s, Pleasanton has become established as an affluent suburban community with a predominantly white-collar job base. The city has continued to attract corporate and tech-industry offices, surviving the downturns of 1991, 2002 and 2009 without any fundamental changes in its economic or social makeup. Despite slow-growth policies enacted in the 1990s, the city's population continued to rise at a rapid pace, from just over fifty thousand residents in 1990 to almost sixty-four thousand in 2000; even in 2010, during the most severe recession the country had seen since the 1930s, Pleasanton's population was nearly seven thousand residents higher than at the previous census, with an influx of tech workers and professionals from East and South Asia bringing greater diversity to the community.

Transit Integration: The Coming of BART and ACE

In 1997, after more than two decades of waiting, the Bay Area Rapid Transit rail system (BART) opened its first station in the Amador-Livermore Valley, serving Dublin and Pleasanton at the northern edge of Hacienda Business Park on a line running through Hayward, Oakland and San Francisco to Daly City. A second station, planned at the same time as the first, opened near Stoneridge Mall in 2011. In 1998, a passenger line called the Altamont Commuter Express (ACE) began operating Stockton–San Jose service on the old Western Pacific tracks, the Southern Pacific tracks having been removed in the 1980s when the company gave up its right-of-way. (Part of that route now forms Railroad Avenue between Main and First in the downtown area.)

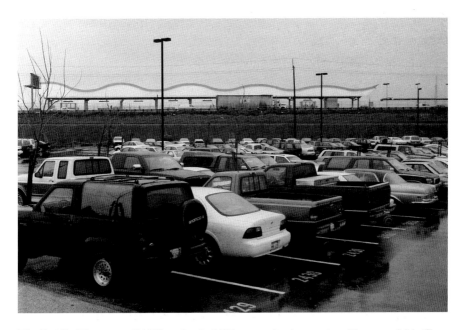

The Dublin/Pleasanton BART station in 1998, soon after its opening. *Museum on Main/Bay Area News Group.*

The Politics of Development

Development issues have continued to play a predominant role in local politics. Ben Tarver, a veteran of the opposition to the Hacienda development, was elected mayor in 1992. Tarver presided over a slow-growth majority on the council, and over the course of the decade, residents approved measures to establish an urban boundary, limit the number of construction permits issued per year and, in 1996, establish a twenty-nine-thousand-unit cap on residential development within city limits.[348]

These successes have created their own difficulties, however. As the Bay Area real estate market heated up over the course of the 2000s, the city's commitment to livable environments and superior schools made it one of the more expensive Bay Area housing markets, while the cap made it more difficult to expand affordable housing at a time of rapidly rising prices. In 2006, a local housing activist (with the aid of an Oakland advocacy group) sued the city for failure to provide its share of the region's affordable housing needs. Although voters reaffirmed their

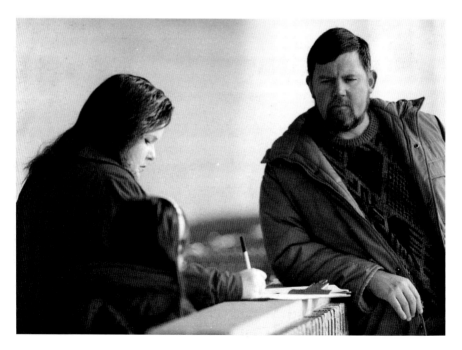

Petition drive to oppose housing developments in Hacienda Business Park, 1992. *Museum on Main/Bay Area News Group.*

commitment to the housing cap in a 2008 referendum, a Superior Court judge determined the ordinance in violation of state law; the city council repealed the cap in 2010 and began working on plans to develop the required lower-income housing.[349]

Historic Preservation

The desire to preserve local landmarks that had developed in the 1970s and '80s continued with both private and public efforts after 1990. Preservation activists campaigned to maintain the appearance of historic houses and buildings, including John Kottinger's adobe barn as well as the "White Corner" that housed Lewis Brothers, Cruikshank & Kolln and Kolln Hardware from the turn of the twentieth century until 2004. The city restored the Alviso Adobe on Foothill Road and opened it as a municipal historic park in the fall of 2008. Heritage and preservation policies continued to evolve as the city established a

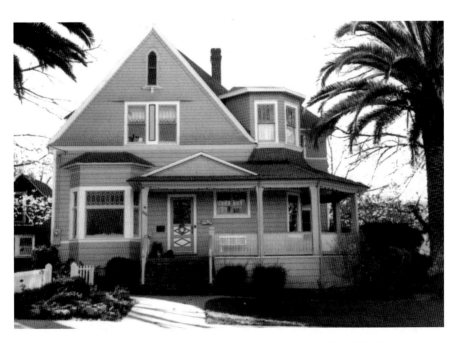

The former E.L. Benedict House at 303 Neal Street, photographed in 1982. Built by Charles Bruce in the 1890s, the home is one of several protected by Pleasanton's historic preservation policies. *Museum on Main.*

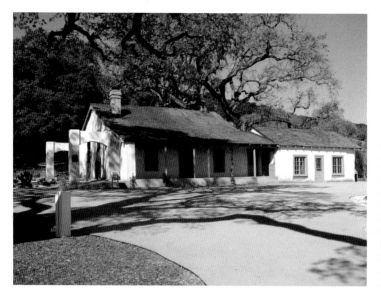

The Francisco Alviso Adobe after its restoration as a historic site park in 2008. *Museum on Main.*

Historic Preservation Task Force in 2011 to consider the issues involved and recommend updates to laws and policies.[350]

Looking Forward

While Pleasanton reaps the benefits of its position within the Bay Area's geography and economy, the "City of Planned Progress" continues to grapple with the delicate balance among environmental sustainability, social responsibility, historic preservation and maintaining a high quality of life for its residents. Recurring issues such as water access and waste disposal will almost certainly raise their heads again, and the challenge of managing growth carefully but fairly will remain as long as the populations of California and the Amador-Livermore Valley continue to rise. With hard work, good luck and some smart decisions, the people of Pleasanton have built an enviable place to live and work—a place, one hopes, ready for whatever twists and turns the future might bring.

NOTES

PART I

1. Jeff Fentress, "Prehistoric Rock Art of Alameda and Contra Costa Counties," in Bean, *Ohlone Past and Present*, 89.
2. Fagan, *Before California*, 53.
3. Ibid., 53–54.
4. Fentress, "Prehistoric Rock Art of Alameda," 67–69.
5. Fagan, *Before California*, 128–42.
6. Ibid., 144–45.
7. Ibid., 136–38.
8. Ibid., 143–44.
9. Wiberg, "Santa Rita Village Mortuary Complex," 49, 61.
10. Fagan, *Before California*, 255.
11. Milliken, *Time of Little Choice*, 13–14.
12. Ibid., 228–29 (map).
13. Ibid., 13.
14. Ibid., 21.
15. Ibid., 28; Beverly O. Ortiz, "Chocheño and Rumsen Narratives: A Comparison," in Bean, *Ohlone Past and Present*, 152–53.
16. Milliken, *Time of Little Choice*, 21–22.
17. DeGrange and DeGrange, *Place Called Sunol*, 6.
18. Milliken, *Time of Little Choice*, 18.

19. Ibid., 19.
20. Ibid., 16–18.
21. Abraham, "Last (and First) Ohlone Basket Weaver."
22. Margolin, *Ohlone Way*, 23–40.
23. Milliken, *Time of Little Choice*, 22–23.
24. Ibid., 24.
25. Ibid., 26–27.
26. Alan Leventhal, Les Field, Hank Alvarez and Rosemary Cambra, "The Ohlone: Back from Extinction," in Bean, *Ohlone Past and Present*, 304; Sandos, *Converting California*, 32.
27. Milliken, *Time of Little Choice*, 28.
28. Ibid.; Ortiz, "Chocheño and Rumsen Narratives," 105–24.
29. Weber, *Spanish Frontier in North America*, 89; Rice, Bullough and Orsi, *Elusive Eden*, 77–83.
30. Sandos, *Converting California*, 3; Weber, *Spanish Frontier in North America*, 239–42.
31. Newton and Bennett, *Fages-Crespi Expedition of 1772*, 21–22.
32. Sandos, *Converting California*, 103; Milliken, *Time of Little Choice*, 135; Lightfoot, *Indians, Missionaries and Merchants*, 82–84.
33. Milliken, *Time of Little Choice*, 62–67.
34. Rice, Bullough and Orsi, *Elusive Eden*, 98–99.
35. Sandos, *Converting California*, 8–10; Lightfoot, *Indians, Missionaries and Merchants*, 59–68.
36. Milliken, *Time of Little Choice*, 90–92; Lightfoot, *Indians, Missionaries and Merchants*, 74–80; Sandos, *Converting California*, 111–27.
37. Lightfoot, *Indians, Missionaries and Merchants*, 63–64.
38. Milliken, *Time of Little Choice*, 115–36.
39. Sandos, *Converting California*, 167–68; Lightfoot, *Indians, Missionaries and Merchants*, 92–95.
40. Sandoval, *Century of Mission San Jose in the East Bay*, 1; Milliken, *Time of Little Choice*, 147.
41. Milliken, *Time of Little Choice*, 269–74.
42. Ibid., 247.
43. Lightfoot, *Indians, Missionaries and Merchants*, 90.
44. Delgado, *Sombras de la Noche*, 2–3.
45. Rice, Bullough and Orsi, *Elusive Eden*, 58–59.
46. Sandos, *Converting California*, 104–5.
47. Rice, Bullough and Orsi, *Elusive Eden*, 132.
48. Ibid., 130.

49. Ibid., 133.
50. Sandoval, *Century of Mission San Jose*, 37.
51. Rice, Bullough and Orsi, *Elusive Eden*, 134.
52. Wood and Munro-Fraser, *History of Alameda County*, 334.
53. Ibid.
54. Delgado, *Sombras de la Noche*, 1–7.
55. Hampson, Duval and Greenwood, *Cultural Resource Investigations*, 14.
56. Rice, Bullough and Orsi, *Elusive Eden*, 137–41.
57. Ibid., 144; Homan, *Historic Livermore, California*, 400.
58. Hagemann, "Juan Pablo Bernal," 185–88.
59. Rice, Bullough and Orsi, *Elusive Eden*, 140–60.
60. Frémont, *Exploring Expedition to the Rocky Mountains*, 429.
61. Hagemann, "Juan Pablo Bernal," 184.
62. Rice, Bullough and Orsi, *Elusive Eden*, 113–27.
63. Ibid., 157–58, 161–62.
64. Hagemann, "Juan Pablo Bernal," 184.
65. Delgado, *Sombras de la Noche*, 8.
66. Rice, Bullough and Orsi, *Elusive Eden*, 218–19.
67. Museum on Main manuscript collection, catalogue no. 2006.021.0237.
68. Wood and Munro-Fraser, *History of Alameda County*, 923.
69. Ibid.
70. Hagemann, "Legal Documents."
71. Hampson, Duval and Greenwood, *Cultural Resource Investigations*, 15–16.
72. Delgado, *Witness to Empire*, 78–79.
73. Wainwright and Museum on Main, *Pleasanton*, 19.
74. Delgado, *Sombras de la Noche*, 15.
75. Hagemann, "Juan Pablo Bernal," 188.
76. Ibid.
77. Ibid., 188–89.
78. *Pleasanton Times*, January 17, 1891.
79. Ibid.
80. Wood and Munro-Fraser, *History of Alameda County*, 166.
81. Ibid., 288–89.
82. Ibid.
83. Lane and Lane, *Amador-Livermore Valley*, 12.
84. Wood and Munro-Fraser, *History of Alameda County*, 876, 923.

Part II

85. Albright, *Official Explorations for Pacific Railroads*, 134–35, 142.
86. Tutorow, *Governor*, 215.
87. Ibid., 259–61.
88. *Daily Alta California*, September 11, 1869.
89. Wood and Munro-Fraser, *History of Alameda County*, 478.
90. *Sacramento Daily Union*, September 9, 1864.
91. Lane and Lane, *Amador-Livermore Valley*, 12.
92. Both the *Sacramento Daily Union* and the *Daily Alta California*, for instance, preferred this spelling.
93. Wainwright and Museum on Main, *Pleasanton*, 23.
94. Wood and Munro-Fraser, *History of Alameda County*, 478–79.
95. U.S. Census, Alameda County, 1860; U.S. Census, Alameda County, Murray Township, 1870.
96. U.S. Census, Alameda County, Murray Township, 1880.
97. *Daily Alta California*, February 1, 1886; *Livermore Herald*, November 16, 1901.
98. Scott, McClure and Boardman, *Referees' Report*.
99. U.S. Census 1860, Alameda County.
100. U.S. Census 1870, Agricultural Production Records, Alameda County, Murray Township.
101. Gibson, "Development of the Livermore Valley Wine District," 39–53.
102. Wait, *Wines and Vines of California*, 165–66.
103. Gibson, "Development of the Livermore Valley Wine District," 60.
104. *Livermore Echo*, September 20 and October 6, 1887.
105. *Pleasanton Times*, August 13, 1910.
106. *San Francisco Call*, February 20, 1909; May 11, 1910; January 1, 1912.
107. *Pacific Rural Press*, February 10, 1894.
108. *Pleasanton Times*, December 21, 1901; November 12, 1904.
109. *San Francisco Call*, June 5, 1895.
110. *Livermore Enterprise*, November 13, 1875; Mosier, "Pleasanton Brick Company."
111. *Livermore Echo*, July 4, 1889; January 2, 1890; and May 15, 1890; Mosier, "Remillard Brick Company."
112. *Livermore Herald*, July 2, 1879.
113. Boessenecker, *Lawman*, 52–53.
114. Wood and Munro-Fraser, *History of Alameda County*, 294.

115. Boessenecker, *Lawman*, 110.
116. Ibid., 57–70, 150–81.
117. McKenney, *McKenney's District Directory for 1879*, 134; *Livermore Herald*, December 27, 1881.
118. Sanborn Fire Insurance Maps, 1888.
119. Halley, *Centennial Year Book of Alameda County*, 500–501.
120. Wood and Munro-Fraser, *History of Alameda County*, 478.
121. *Daily Alta California*, March 28, 1869.
122. McKenney, *McKenney's District Directory for 1879*, 132–35; *Livermore Herald*, January 1, 1879.
123. *Livermore Herald*, September 16, 1880.
124. Sanborn Fire Insurance Maps, 1888, 1898, 1907.
125. Berry, Pleasanton City Council minutes, June 7, 1895.
126. *Sacramento Daily Union*, March 17, 1874.
127. Long and the Pleasanton School History Committee, *Echoes of School Bells*, 7; *Pleasanton Times*, August 13, 1910; *Progressive Pleasanton 1902*, 7.
128. *Pleasanton Star*, June 6, 1885.
129. *Progressive Pleasanton 1902*, 7.
130. Homann, *Historic Livermore, California*, 289.
131. *Sacramento Daily Union*, September 1, 1876.
132. Ibid., June 5, 1882; Wainwright and Museum on Main, *Pleasanton*, 51.
133. Wood and Munro-Fraser, *History of Alameda County*, 473.
134. Ibid., 481.
135. *Livermore Herald*, February 19, 1880.
136. *San Francisco Call*, September 27, 1890; April 27, 1899.
137. Berry, Pleasanton City Council minutes, February 2, 1903.
138. Goulart, *Holy Ghost Festas*, 228; *San Francisco Call*, October 4, 1896.
139. *Livermore Echo*, June 28, 1888; November 14, 1889.
140. *Pleasanton Star*, June 6, 1885.
141. Pleasanton Fire Department Annual Report, 1967.
142. *Livermore Echo*, July 4, 1889; Sanborn Fire Insurance Maps, 1893.
143. *Livermore Herald*, May 13, 1880; July 15, 1880.
144. *Sacramento Daily Union*, April 22, 1879; May 9, 1879.
145. *Livermore Herald*, July 1, 1880; October 4, 1880; *Daily Alta California*, September 4, 1871.
146. Robinson, *Hearsts*, 171, dates the purchase 1881 but doesn't provide a citation; the *Livermore Echo* ran a story about Hearst purchasing "the R.M. Fitzgerald ranch near Sunol" on April 4, 1889, after a February 14 story claimed that he sought a property in the area.

147. Wait, *Wines and Vines of California*, 155–66; *Daily Alta California*, November 10, 1887; *Sacramento Daily Union*, August 18, 1892.
148. Greenberg, "Growth and Conflict at the Suburban Fringe," 47–51; Hampson, Duval and Greenwood, *Cultural Resource Investigations*, 18–22.
149. Leventhal, Field, Alvarez and Cambra, "Ohlone," 308–9.
150. Lightfoot, *Indians, Missionaries and Merchants*, 220.
151. Robinson, *Hearsts*, 243–44, 248, 254–56.
152. Ibid., 364–67.
153. Leventhal, Field, Alvarez and Cambra, "Ohlone," 309–12.
154. Jordan, "Proctor Knott's Speech on Duluth," 67–78.
155. *San Francisco Call*, May 15, 1891; February 27, 1894.
156. Henning, General Laws of the State of California, 744–49, 899–910.
157. *Livermore Echo*, April 26, 1894; Pleasanton incorporation documents, June 11, 1894.
158. *San Francisco Call*, May 1, 1894.
159. Berry, Pleasanton City Council minutes, June 22, 1894.
160. Ibid., August 8, 1894.
161. Ibid., September 3, 1894; January 7, 1895.
162. Ibid., March 4, 1901; March 26, 1901.
163. Sanborn Fire Insurance Maps. *Pleasanton, Alameda County, California*.
164. *Pleasanton Times*, May 26, 1898.
165. Berry, Pleasanton City Council minutes, April 18, 1898.
166. Ibid., December 18, 1899.
167. Ibid., December 2, 1901.
168. See *Livermore Herald*, October 19, 1901, for an example.
169. Ibid., August 7, 1916.
170. Ibid., April 2, 1919.
171. Ibid., January 7, 1895.
172. Ibid., May 3, 1909.
173. Ibid., March 18, 1918.
174. Ibid., March 13–July 6, 1896.
175. Ibid., October 21, 1912; Council Resolution no. 554, February 7, 1913.
176. *Livermore Herald*, November 2, 1912; March 15, 1913.
177. Ibid., May 24, 1902.
178. Ibid., July 5, 1902.
179. *Pleasanton Times*, August 13, 1910.
180. Berry, Pleasanton City Council minutes, December 2, 1912.

181. Ibid., February 24, 1914.
182. Ibid., June 30, 1914; July 20, 1914.
183. *San Francisco Call*, September 1, 1896.
184. *Pleasanton Times*, January 21, 1893.
185. *Pleasanton Bulletin*, September 25, 1897; January 22, 1898.
186. *San Francisco Call*, December 6, 1910.
187. Berry, Pleasanton City Council minutes, September 3, 1907.
188. *Pleasanton Times*, June 13, 1908.
189. Hofsommer, *Southern Pacific*, 46–47.
190. *Livermore Herald*, February 17, 1906; March 3, 1906.
191. *San Francisco Call*, June 10, 1912.
192. *Pleasanton Times*, June 13, 1908.
193. Homann, *Historic Livermore, California*, 226–27.
194. *Livermore Herald*, August 3, 1928.
195. Ibid., January 23, 1915.
196. Berry, Pleasanton City Council minutes, August 1, 1907; August 5, 1912.
197. *Pleasanton Times*, November 24, 1917.
198. *San Francisco Call*, June 4, 1900; June 28, 1908.
199. *Pleasanton Times*, November 12, 1904.
200. Sanborn Fire Insurance Maps, *Pleasanton, Alameda County, California*.
201. Ibid., 1898.
202. U.S. Census 1900, Alameda County, Murray Township.
203. *Pacific Rural Press*, September 27, 1873.
204. *San Francisco Call*, March 16, 1898.
205. *Pleasanton Times*, August 13, 1910.
206. Berry, Pleasanton City Council minutes, October 25, 1897; February 24, 1898.
207. *Livermore Herald*, September 4, 1915.
208. Ibid., November 17, 1900; *Sacramento Daily Union*, August 26, 1898.
209. Berry, Pleasanton City Council minutes, February 1–March 1, 1897.
210. *Livermore Herald*, November 20, 1897.
211. *Progressive Pleasanton 1902*, 22–23.
212. *San Francisco Call*, April 28, 1912.
213. Ibid., July 16, 1904; August 12, 1909; July 25, 1911; and July 25, 1912.
214. Ibid., July 7, 1902.
215. *Pacific Rural Press*, September 6, 1902.
216. *San Francisco Call*, April 22, 1912.

217. *Livermore Herald*, June 29, 1912; *San Francisco Call*, July 8, 1912.
218. *San Francisco Call*, October 23–27, 1912.
219. Christian, *Alameda County Fair*, 16.
220. Berry, Pleasanton City Council minutes, May 6, June 3 and August 5, 1918.
221. *Pleasanton Times*, May 18, 1918.
222. Ibid., January 31, 1920.
223. Council Resolution 689b, May 14, 1917.
224. Berry, Pleasanton City Council minutes, November 4, 1918.
225. Robinson, *Hearsts*, 377–80.
226. U.S. Census, 1910 and 1920.
227. Greenberg, "Growth and Conflict at the Suburban Fringe," 46.
228. *Livermore Herald*, October 21, 1938.
229. Hampson, Duval and Greenwood, *Cultural Resource Investigations*, 22–25; Wainwright and Museum on Main, *Pleasanton*, 67.
230. California State Mining Bureau, *Report of the State Mineralogist*, 37.
231. *Livermore Herald*, July 27, 1923.
232. *Pleasanton Times*, June 27, 1930.
233. *Livermore Herald*, May 12, 1917.
234. *Pleasanton Times*, February 22, 1929.
235. Long and the Pleasanton School History Committee, *Echoes of School Bells*, 27–30.
236. *Pleasanton Times*, August 17, 1923.
237. *Livermore Herald*, May 16, 1924.
238. Ibid., February 16, 1940.
239. Ibid., May 3, 1940.
240. Rice, Bullough and Orsi, *Elusive Eden*, 417.
241. Pleasanton Ordinance 130, March 19, 1923.
242. *Daily Alta California*, June 28, 1874.
243. *Sacramento Daily Union*, March 25, 1871.
244. Gibson, "Development of the Livermore Valley Wine District," 61–62.
245. See extant issues of the *Pleasanton Times*, *Livermore Herald* or any other local newspaper between 1925 and 1932.
246. *Pleasanton Times*, December 29, 1922.
247. Ibid., February 17, 1927.
248. Ibid., August 2, 1929.
249. *Pleasanton Times*, June 8, 1932; March 3, 1933; October 27, 1933; and April 13, 1934.
250. *Livermore Herald*, July 22, 1932.

251. *Pleasanton News*, August 26, 1932.
252. *Southern Alameda County News*, June 13, 1935 (front page reproduced in *Tri-Valley News*, Special Section, February 24, 1974).
253. *Pleasanton Times*, February 6, 1931.
254. Ibid., August 7, 1931.
255. Ibid., July 22, 1932.
256. Homann, *Historic Livermore, California*, 222–24.
257. *Pleasanton Times*, April 7, 1933.
258. Ibid., June 10, 1931.
259. Berry, Pleasanton City Council minutes, April 3, 1933.
260. *Pleasanton Times*, January 15, 1932.
261. Ibid., April 14–21, 1933; Rice, Bullough and Orsi, *Elusive Eden*, 436–38.
262. *Pleasanton Times*, January 20, 1934; Berry, Pleasanton City Council minutes, August 6, 1934.
263. *Pleasanton Times*, October 2, 1931.
264. Ibid., April 11, 1930.
265. Ibid., July 8, 1932.
266. Ibid., March 11, 1932.
267. Ibid., July 7, 1933.
268. *Livermore Herald*, September 13, 1935.
269. Christian, *Alameda County Fair*, 18.
270. *Livermore Herald*, July 7, 1939.
271. Christian, *Alameda County Fair*, 19.
272. Minniear and Vonheeder-Leopold, *Dublin and the Tri-Valley*, 7–8.
273. U.S. Census 1940.
274. Rice, Bullough and Orsi, *Elusive Eden*, 458, 479–80.
275. *Pleasanton Times*, February 20, 1942.
276. *Livermore Herald*, April 24–May 8, 1942.
277. Rice, Bullough and Orsi, *Elusive Eden*, 477.
278. *Pleasanton Times*, July 21, 1944.
279. Hagemann, *History of the City of Pleasanton*, 46.
280. *Pleasanton Times*, September 23, 1943.
281. Decoraro, *Pleasanton's War Casualties*, 3.
282. Minniear and Vonheeder-Leopold, *Dublin and the Tri-Valley*, 46.

Part III

283. Ibid., 109.
284. Greenberg, "Growth and Conflict at the Suburban Fringe," 104–6.
285. Ibid., 107–8.
286. Ibid., 125–26.
287. *Pleasanton Times*, March 1, 1956.
288. Greenberg, "Growth and Conflict at the Suburban Fringe," 78–79.
289. *Livermore Herald*, May 15, 1942; Sanborn Fire Insurance Maps, 1943.
290. *Pleasanton Times*, April 14, 1950; *Livermore Herald*, September 22, 1950.
291. *Livermore Herald*, April 20, 1956.
292. Berry, Pleasanton City Council minutes, April 6, 1953.
293. Pleasanton City Ordinance 228, February 1, 1954.
294. Long and the Pleasanton School History Committee, *Echoes of School Bells*, 86.
295. Greenberg, "Growth and Conflict at the Suburban Fringe," 131–32.
296. Ibid., 131–32.
297. Ibid., 145–46.
298. Ibid., 139–45.
299. Ibid., 146.
300. Ibid., 130, 133–34, 145.
301. Ibid., 217.
302. Ibid., 217–26.
303. *Pleasanton Times*, January 23, 1963.
304. Greenberg, "Growth and Conflict at the Suburban Fringe," 224–28.
305. Ibid., 229.
306. Ibid., 219–20.
307. Ibid., 246.
308. Ibid., 220, 244–45.
309. Ibid., 154.
310. Ibid., 155.
311. Ibid., 221.
312. Ibid., 234.
313. Ibid., 236–38.
314. Berry, Pleasanton City Council minutes, August 13, 1956.
315. City of Pleasanton, Annual Report, 1964.
316. Berry, Pleasanton City Council minutes, October 15, 1962; *Pleasanton Times*, August 21, 1968.

317. Berry, Pleasanton City Council minutes, March 22, 1965.
318. Greenberg, "Growth and Conflict at the Suburban Fringe," 117–18.
319. Ibid., 156–57.
320. Ibid., 161–67.
321. *Amador-Livermore Valley Historical Society Bulletin* 1, no. 1.
322. *Amador-Livermore Valley Historical Society Bulletin* 7, no. 2.
323. Greenberg, "Growth and Conflict at the Suburban Fringe," 106–8.
324. Edmands, "Atom in Our Town," 8–9.
325. *Pleasanton Times*, April 14, 1950.
326. Berry, Pleasanton City Council minutes, August 14, 1961.
327. *Livermore News*, November 20, 1952.
328. *Livermore Herald-News*, August 26, 1969.
329. Greenberg, "Growth and Conflict at the Suburban Fringe," 285–86.
330. Ibid., 292–93.
331. Ibid., 288–99, 293.
332. Ibid., 332–33.
333. Ibid., 298–303.
334. Ibid., 303–11.
335. Ibid., 294.
336. Ibid., 333–34.
337. Ibid., 347–62.
338. Ibid., 360–61.
339. Pleasanton General Plan, "Growth Management Element," 1978, 6.
340. Wainwright and Museum on Main, *Pleasanton*, 127.
341. Long and the Pleasanton School History Committee, *Echoes of School Bells*, 97–101.
342. Bean, "Introduction," *Ohlone Past and Present*, xxiv; Leventhal, Field, Alvarez and Cambra, "Ohlone," 298–99.
343. Greenberg, "Growth and Conflict at the Suburban Fringe," 426.
344. Ibid., 429–30.
345. Ibid., 430–41.
346. Ibid., 400–1.
347. Ibid., 418–24.
348. *San Francisco Chronicle*, January 31, 2010, Tarver obituary.
349. *Contra Costa Times*, July 18, 2010.
350. Berry, Pleasanton City Council minutes, December 6, 2011.

BIBLIOGRAPHY

Newspapers

Livermore Herald, various issues, 1879–83. Accessed via California Digital Newspaper Collection.
Pleasanton Bulletin, various issues, 1897–98.
Pleasanton News, various issues, 1932.
Pleasanton Star, various issues, 1885–87.
Pleasanton Times, various issues, 1888–1974.
Sacramento Daily Union, various issues, 1861–79. Accessed via California Digital Newspaper Collection.
San Francisco Call, various issues, 1900–1913. Accessed via California Digital Newspaper Collection.
(San Francisco) *Daily Alta California*, various issues, 1851–89. Accessed via California Digital Newspaper Collection.
(San Francisco) *Pacific Rural Press*, various issues, 1871–1916. Accessed via California Digital Newspaper Collection.

Maps

King, M.G. *Oakland Daily & Weekly Tribune Map of Alameda County*. Oakland, CA: Tribune Publishing Company, 1880.

Sanborn Fire Insurance Maps. *Pleasanton, Alameda County, California*. New York: Sanborn Map Company, 1888–1943.

Books and Articles

Abraham, Kera. "The Last (and First) Ohlone Basket Weaver: Seaside Artist Resurrects a Long-Lost Native Craft," *Monterey County Weekly*. http://www.montereycountyweekly.com/news/cover/seaside-artist-resurrects-a-long-lost-native-craft/article_8b5eea0f-89b2-50df-b96e-fb66dc4b833f.html.

Albright, George Leslie. *Official Explorations for Pacific Railroads, 1853–1855*. Berkeley: University of California Press, 1921.

Bean, John Lowell, ed. *The Ohlone Past and Present: Native Americans of the San Francisco Bay Region*. Menlo Park, CA: Ballena Press, 1994.

Boessenecker, John. *Gold Dust & Gunsmoke: Tales of Gold Rush Outlaws, Gunfighters, Lawmen, and Vigilantes*. New York: John Wiley & Sons, 1999.

———. *Lawman: The Life and Times of Harry Morse, 1835–1912*. Norman: University of Oklahoma Press, 1998.

Christian, Victoria. *Alameda County Fair: Images of America*. Charleston, SC: Arcadia Press, 2011.

———. *Sunol: Images of America*. Charleston, SC: Arcadia Press, 2007.

Decoraro, John. *Pleasanton's War Casualties: World War II and Beyond*. Pleasanton, CA: self-published, 2010.

DeGrange, Connie, and Allen DeGrange. *A Place Called Sunol*. Sunol, CA: DeGrange Publishing, 1995.

Delgado, James P. *Sombras de la Noche: The Agustin Bernal Adobe, Its Inhabitants and Heritage*. San Jose, CA: Smith & McKay Printing Company, 1976.

———. *Witness to Empire: The Life of Antonio Maria Suñol*. San Jose: Sourisseau Academy for California State and Local History, San Jose State University, 1977.

Edmands, John. "The Atom in Our Town: Pleasanton, California." *Citizen Atom, New York Times* advertising supplement, December 11, 1960, 8–9.

Fagan, Brian. *Before California: An Archaeologist Looks at Our Earliest Inhabitants*. Walnut Creek, CA: AltaMira Press, 2003.

Frémont, John C. *The Exploring Expedition to the Rocky Mountains, Oregon, and California*. Buffalo, NY: George H. Derby and Company, 1852.

Gibson, David J. "The Development of the Livermore Valley Wine District." MA thesis, University of California–Davis, 1969.

Goldsmith, Paul. "Putting Land through the Wringer." *Sunset Magazine* 23, no. 4 (1909): 433–34.

Goulart, Tony, ed. *The Holy Ghost Festas: A Historic Perspective of the Portuguese in California*. San Jose: Portuguese Chamber of Commerce of California, 2002.

Greenberg, Douglas. "Growth and Conflict at the Suburban Fringe: The Case of the Livermore-Amador Valley." PhD dissertation, University of California–Berkeley, 1986.

Hagemann, Herbert L., Jr. *A History of the City of Pleasanton: Centennial Celebration June 18, 1994*. Pleasanton, CA: Amador-Livermore Valley Historical Society, 1993.

———. "Juan Pablo Bernal." *Pacific Historian* 8, no. 4 (November 1964): 181–92.

———. "Legal Documents Relating to the Granting of Rancho El Valle de San Jose." *Pacific Historian* 9, no. 3 (August 1965): 147–52.

———. "Rancho El Valle de San Jose—Abstract of Title." *Pacific Historian* 9, no. 2 (May 1965): 107–9.

Halley, William. *Centennial Yearbook of Alameda County*. Oakland, CA: William Halley, 1876.

Hampson, R. Paul, Charlene Duval and Roberta S. Greenwood. *Cultural Resource Investigations at Alviso Adobe Community Park*. Pacific Palisades, CA: Greenwood and Associates, 2000.

Hofsommer, Don L. *The Southern Pacific, 1901–1985*. College Station: Texas A&M University Press, 2009.

Homann, Anne Marshall. *Historic Livermore, California: Illustrated A–Z*. Walnut Creek, CA: Hardscratch Press, 2007.

Jordan, Philip D. "Proctor Knott's Speech on Duluth." *Minnesota History* 34, no. 2 (Summer 1954): 67–78.

Lane, Bob, and Pat Lane. *The Amador-Livermore Valley: A Pictorial History*. Norfolk, VA: Donning Press, 1988.

———. *Celebrating Family Fun at the County Fair!* Pleasanton, CA: Alameda County Agricultural Fair Association, 2002.

Lightfoot, Kent G. *Indians, Missionaries and Merchants: The Legacy of Colonial Encounters on the California Frontiers*. Berkeley: University of California Press, 2005.

Long, Jerri, and the Pleasanton School History Committee. *Echoes of School Bells: A History of Amador-Pleasanton Public Schools.* Livermore, CA: Quali-Type Inc., 1989.

Margolin, Malcolm. *The Ohlone Way: Indian Life in the San Francisco-Monterey Bay Area.* Berkeley, CA: Heyday Press, 1978.

McKenney, L.M. *McKenney's District Directory for 1879, of Alameda, Contra Costa, San Mateo, Santa Cruz, San Benito and Monterey Counties, Including All Residents, with Sketch of Cities and Towns.* San Francisco, CA: L.M. McKenney, 1878.

Milliken, Randall. *A Time of Little Choice: The Disintegration of Tribal Culture in the San Francisco Bay Area, 1769–1810.* Menlo Park, CA: Ballena Press, 1995.

Minniear, Steven S., and Georgean Vonheeder-Leopold. *Dublin and the Tri-Valley: The World War II Years: Images of America.* Charleston, SC: Arcadia Press, 2014.

Newton, Janet. *Stories of the Vineyards and Wineries of the Livermore Valley.* 2nd edition. Livermore, CA: self-published, 1987.

Newton, Janet, and Virginia Bennett. *The Fages-Crespi Expedition of 1772.* Pleasanton, CA: Amador-Livermore Valley Historical Society, 1972.

Progressive Pleasanton 1902. Pleasanton, CA: Pleasanton Times, 1902.

Rice, Richard B., William A. Bullough and Richard J. Orsi. *The Elusive Eden: A New History of California.* 3rd edition. New York: McGraw-Hill, 2002.

Robinson, Judith. *The Hearsts: An American Dynasty.* San Francisco, CA: Telegraph Hill Press, 1991.

Sandos, James A. *Converting California: Indians and Franciscans in the Missions.* New Haven, CT: Yale University Press, 2004.

Sandoval, John. *A Century of Mission San Jose in the East Bay.* Hayward, CA: Chapel of the Chimes, n.d.

Stuart, Reginald R., and Grace D. Stuart. *Corridor Country: An Interpretive History of the Amador-Livermore Valley.* Vol. 1, *The Spanish-Mexican Period.* Pleasanton, CA: Amador-Livermore Valley Historical Society, 1966.

Thompson & West. *Official and Historical Atlas Map of Alameda County, California.* Oakland, CA: Thompson & West, 1878.

Tutorow, Norman E. *The Governor: The Life and Legacy of Leland Stanford.* Glendale, CA: Arthur H. Clark Company, 2004.

Wainwright, Mary-Jo, and the Museum on Main. *Pleasanton: Images of America.* Charleston, SC: Arcadia Press, 2007.

Wait, Frona Eunice. *Wines and Vines of California: A Treatise on the Ethics of Wine Drinking.* San Francisco, CA: Bancroft Company, 1889.

Weber, David J. *The Spanish Frontier in North America*. New Haven, CT: Yale University Press, 1992.

Wiberg, Randy. "The Santa Rita Village Mortuary Complex: Evidence and Implications of a Meganos Intrusion." MA thesis, San Francisco State University, 1984.

Wood, M.W., and J.P. Munro-Fraser. *History of Alameda County, California*. Oakland, CA: M.W. Wood, 1883.

OTHER MATERIALS

Architectural Resources Group. Pleasanton Downtown Historic Context Statement (draft), September 2012. Accessed at http://www.cityofpleasantonca.gov/pdf/Pleasanton_Context_Statement-DRAFT.pdf.

Berry, Terry. Unpublished notes on Pleasanton town and city council minutes, 1894–1967. Museum on Main collection (uncatalogued).

Bunshah, Barbara, and Don Meeker. Indices to Livermore newspapers, 1875–1965. Contained in digitized PDF files derived from bound typescript in the collections of the Livermore Public Library and the Livermore Heritage Guild.

California State Mining Bureau. *Report of the State Mineralogist* 17 (1921).

Henning, W.F. *General Laws of the State of California, as Amended and in Force at the Close of the Thirty-sixth Session of the Legislature, 1905*. San Francisco, CA, 1908.

Minutes of the Pleasanton City Council, 1969–present. Accessed via www.cityofpleasantonca.gov.

Minutes of the Pleasanton Fire Department, 1901–38. Transcribed in unpublished form by Ted Klenk. Museum on Main collection (uncatalogued).

Mosier, Dan. "Pleasanton Brick Company." California Bricks. http://calbricks.netfirms.com/brick.black.html.

———. "Remillard Brick Company." California Bricks. http://calbricks.netfirms.com/brick.pleasanton.html.

Scott, Joseph, Richard A. McClure and William F. Boardman. *Referees' Report in the Case of Augustine Bernal and Juana Higuera Bernal, His Wife, Plaintiffs, v. Juan Pablo Bernal et al., Defendants*, 1866. Museum on Main MS 2006.021.0318d.

Bibliography

United States Census Records, 1860–1940. Accessed via Ancestry.com. Transcriptions of 1870 and 1880 Alameda County censuses available at Livermore-Amador Genealogical Society website, www.l-ags.org/databases.html. Transcription of 1860 Alameda County census accessed at http://files.usgwarchives.net/ca/alameda/census/1860/alameda/alameda.txt.

INDEX

A

Agricultural District Fair 89
agriculture 16, 17, 25, 45, 47, 88, 113
  fruit and vegetable 95, 113, 115
  grain 45, 53, 85, 95
  hops 46, 47, 95
  sugar beets 47, 79, 95, 113, 115
Alameda County 34, 47, 50, 71, 82, 87, 89, 102, 103, 104, 106, 107, 111, 123, 125, 139
Alameda County Fair 88, 89, 91, 92, 94, 110, 112, 122, 134, 142
Alisal Ranchería 32, 37, 38, 39, 43, 58, 65, 66, 67, 144
Alviso, Francisco 25, 30, 85, 95
Amador, Jose Maria 22, 25, 30
Amador-Livermore Valley 9, 10, 11, 14, 15, 19, 22, 23, 26, 27, 31, 32, 34, 38, 63, 64, 74, 76, 82, 115, 129, 134, 137, 149
Amador-Livermore Valley Historical Society 133, 142
Arendt family 46, 56, 60, 106, 107
Arendt, Henry 53
automobiles 82, 83, 94, 97, 100, 120

B

Benedict, Elsie 91
Bernal, Agustin 19, 27, 43, 44, 49, 63, 65, 66, 67
Bernal family 25, 32, 45, 65
Bernal, Juan Pablo 25, 26, 27, 28, 30, 32, 45
Bernal y Kottinger, Maria Refugia 28, 32, 41
Bernal y Neal, Angela 42
Bilz, J.A. 56, 60
Binder, William 77
Bojorques, Narciso 50, 53
brickmaking 50, 84, 95
Bruce, C.A. 77
Bustamante, Tomas Procopio 50

C

Californios 21, 22, 23, 42, 43, 53, 110
Camp Parks 112, 117, 119
Camp Shoemaker 112, 118, 119
Castlewood Country Club 101, 135, 138
cattle 16, 25, 28, 32, 35, 45, 53, 85

INDEX

Cope, J. Hal 72, 73, 79, 91
Crespi, Juan 15

D

dairies and dairying 44, 85, 86, 95, 106, 125, 129
Donnally, M.C. 72, 76
Dougherty Station. *See* Dublin
Dublin 11, 22, 38, 64, 76, 82, 99, 112, 117, 125, 126, 132, 134, 139, 149
Duerr, Charles 43, 54

F

Fages, Pedro 15
Feliz y Bernal, Rafaela 24, 32
films and filmmaking 97, 99
Franciscan Order 15, 16, 17, 20
Freemasons 60, 61
Frémont, John C. 27

G

gravel and aggregate mining 97, 121
Guadalupe Hidalgo, Treaty of 27, 28

H

Hacienda Business Park 144, 147, 149, 150
Hacienda de Pozo de Verona 67, 101, 135
Hearst, George 63, 67
Hearst, Phoebe Apperson 63, 70, 77, 94, 133
Hearst, William Randolph 67, 101
Higuera y Bernal, Maria Juana (later Nevis) 24, 49
horse racing 49, 87, 88, 89, 109, 110
horses 16, 17, 19, 25, 26, 27, 33, 45, 49, 58, 63, 67, 72, 89, 91, 95, 107, 109, 111
Hortenstine, John B. 56, 60, 72, 79
hotels 54, 56, 60, 64, 72, 97, 121
housing 115, 117, 120, 126, 127, 129, 147, 148, 150

I

immigrant groups
  Chinese 43, 44, 49, 50, 58, 84, 94, 113
  Danish 44
  German 43, 114
  Japanese 49, 95, 113, 114
  Mexican 42, 115
  Portuguese 44, 49, 61, 94
influenza 93, 94
International Order of Odd Fellows (IOOF) 60
Irmandades do Divino Espirito Santo (IDES) 44, 61

J

Jackson and Perkins 95
Junior Chamber of Commerce (Jaycees) 107, 109

K

Kolb, Philip 56, 74, 75, 76
Kolln Hardware 56, 151
Kottinger, John W. 33, 34, 35, 37, 38, 41, 42, 46, 54, 56, 57, 60, 133, 151

L

Lawrence Livermore National Laboratory (LLNL) 119, 127, 134, 135, 139
libraries, public 73, 77, 131, 144
Lions Club International 107
Livermore-Amador Valley Water Management Agency (LAVWMA) 140
Livermore (city) 38, 42, 44, 46, 52, 58, 60, 62, 64, 71, 76, 79, 81, 82, 85, 89, 95, 97, 103, 107, 110, 112, 119, 124, 129, 135, 137, 138, 139
Livermore, Robert 26, 30, 42

INDEX

M

Mexican Republic 20, 25, 27
Mission San Jose 19, 21, 22, 23, 65
Mission Santa Clara 19
Morse, Harry 35, 50, 53
Murray Township 34, 35, 37, 42, 43, 44, 45, 50, 52, 57, 58, 64, 75, 76, 132
Murrieta, Joaquin 32, 33, 34, 50

N

Neal, J.H. 72, 76
Neal, Joshua A. 42, 57, 76
Nevis, Joseph 44, 49, 72, 87
newspapers
  Independent 139
  Livermore Herald 50, 74, 103, 139
  Pleasanton Bulletin 61, 73, 86
  Pleasanton News 105
  Pleasanton Star 61, 71
  Pleasanton Times 33, 61, 86, 105, 125, 135, 139
  Southern Alameda County News 105
Niles Canyon 32, 38, 54, 64, 82, 105, 138
Nusbaumer, Louis 43, 54, 89

O

Ohlone 10, 11, 12, 13, 14, 16, 65, 67, 144
Old Hearst Ranch 135. *See* Castlewood Country Club

P

Pacheco, Jose Dolores 23, 30
Palmer, J.R. 56, 60, 72
Parks, Norman H. 105, 107
Pico, Antonio Maria 23, 26, 30, 45
Pleasanton Chamber of Commerce 81, 82, 140
Pleasanton (city) 70
  annexations 125, 126
  economy 45, 46, 47, 49, 50, 53, 56, 79, 94, 95, 103, 106, 109, 119, 129, 140, 145, 146
  fire department 61, 72, 97, 130, 135
  founding 37, 41, 42
  incorporation 71
  Main Street Arch 109
  name, origins of 42
  parks 73, 79, 142
  police 130
  politics 44, 63, 72, 73, 75, 86, 102, 106, 127, 132, 137, 138, 139, 141, 146, 150
  population 42, 71, 76, 94, 122, 130, 148
  schools. *See* schools
  town hall 72, 77, 131, 142
Pleasanton Township 76, 93, 106, 113, 117, 120
Pleasonton, Alfred 42
Procopio. *See* Bustamante, Tomas Procopio
Prohibition 79, 94, 95, 102, 103, 105, 109

R

railroads 38, 41, 42, 43, 45, 46, 53, 62, 64, 82, 83, 94, 97, 99
  Altamont Commuter Express (ACE) 149
  Bay Area Rapid Transit (BART) 149
  Southern Pacific 67, 82
  Western Pacific (1862-70) 38
  Western Pacific (1903-83) 82
Rancho Las Positas 23
Rancho San Ramón 22, 23, 25, 30
Rancho Santa Rita 23, 30, 64, 65
Rancho Santa Teresa 23, 24, 25, 31
Rancho Valle de San José 23, 25, 28, 30, 37, 44, 63
roads and highways 35, 38, 82, 83, 97, 100, 106, 107, 120, 127

S

saloons and bars 54, 56, 76, 93, 94, 103
San Jose (city) 23, 24, 25, 28, 32, 33, 34, 38, 41, 53, 58, 60, 129, 149
San Ramon (city) 82, 89
San Ramon Valley 15, 19, 22, 38
San Ramon Village (development) 124, 125
schools 57, 58, 63, 120, 147, 150
   Alisal Elementary School 120
   Amador Valley High School 99, 101, 115, 123
   California State College (later University), Hayward (later East Bay) 123
   Foothill High School 142
   Harvest Park Middle School 142
   Livermore Union High School 58, 99
   Pleasanton Grammar School 58, 101
   Pleasanton Middle School 121
   Valley View Elementary School 120
   Walnut Grove Elementary School 142
Shoemaker Naval Hospital 112, 118, 119
Silver family 44, 89
Soto, Juan 50, 53
Spain and the Spanish 10, 11, 14, 15, 16, 17, 19, 20
Stoneridge Mall 145, 149
Suñol, Antonio Maria 23, 27, 30, 45
Sunol (city) 53, 58, 62, 64, 76, 89, 101, 148
Sunol Valley 11, 34

V

Valley Community Services District (VCSD) 124, 125, 126, 132, 137, 138, 139
Vasquez, Tiburcio 50, 53
Volk-McLain (developers) 124, 125

W

Warren, Earl 103
Washington Township 64, 105, 107, 132, 138
water, wastewater and sewage 15, 45, 47, 64, 70, 72, 73, 74, 75, 91, 105, 112, 124, 126, 132, 135, 137, 138, 139, 140, 147, 152
wine and wineries 46, 63, 94, 103, 109
Women's Improvement Club 77, 79, 81, 107, 121, 131
World War I 91, 94
World War II 112, 113, 114, 124

Z

Zone 7 water district 132, 137, 139, 140

ABOUT THE AUTHOR

Ken MacLennan joined the Museum on Main staff in 2008, shortly after completing his MA in museum studies at San Francisco State University. He also holds an MA in history from the University of Illinois at Urbana–Champaign, where he worked in exhibit development for the Spurlock Museum of World Cultures. Mr. MacLennan is a member of the American Alliance of Museums, the California Association of Museums and the Society for Military History.

The Museum on Main was established in 1970 by the Amador-Livermore Valley Historical Society to preserve and promote the history of the Tri-Valley region through public programming, which includes exhibits, lectures, school tours and annual events.

Visit us at
www.historypress.net

This title is also available as an e-book